The Liberals in Power in Alberta
1905-1921

By the Authors

By Austin Mardon A Conspectus of the Contribution of Herodotus to the Development of Geographical Thought 1990;
International Law and Space Rescue Systems 1991;
Kensington Stone and Other Essays 1991;
A Transient in Whirl 1991;
Alone Against the Revolution 1996;
Political Networks in Alberta 1905-1992 2002;
7 days in Moscow 2005;
The Contribution of Geography to the Recovery of Antarctic Meteorites 2005;

By Ernest Mardon Narrative
Unity of the Cursor Mundi 1967;
The Founding Faculty of the University of Lethbridge 1968;
Place Names of Southern Alberta 1970;
The Conflict Between the Individual & Society in the Plays of James Bridie 1971;
Who's Who in Federal Politics from Alberta Ridings 1972;
English Studies at Canadian Universities 1972;
Community Names of Alberta 1975

By Austin Mardon & Ernest Mardon
Alberta Judicial Biographical Dictionary 1990;
Alberta Ethnic Mormon Politicians 1991;
Alberta Ethnic German Politicians 1991;
When Kitty Met the Ghost 1991;
Down & Out & On the Run in Moscow 1991;
The Girl Who Could Walk Through Walls 1991;
Alberta Mormon Politicians 1992;
Alberta General Election Returns & Subsequent By-elections 1882-1992 1993;
Edmonton Political Biography 1994;
Alberta Political Biographical Dictionary 1994;
Alberta Executive Council 1905-1990 1994;
Early Christian Saints 1997;
Later Christian Saints for Children 1997;
Many Christian Saints for Children 1997;
Childhood Memories & Legends of Christmas Past 1998;
Community Names of Alberta 1999;
Men of Dawn 1999;
United Farmers of Alberta 1999;
The Genealogy of the Mardon Family 2000;
Alberta Catholic Politicians 2000; Alberta Anglican Politicians 2001;
Liberal Politicians in Alberta 1905-1992 2002;
What's in a Name? 2002;
Edmonton Members of the Legislature 2004

Ernest G. Mardon & Austin A. Mardon

The Liberals in Power in Alberta 1905-1921

Edited by Claire MacMaster

Golden Meteorite Press

A Golden Meteorite Press Book.

© 2012 copyright by Austin Mardon & Ernest Mardon, Canada.

All rights reserved. No part of this work may be reproduced in any form or by any means, electronic or mechanical, including photocopying, recording, taping, or any retrieval system, without the written permission of Golden Meteorite Press at: aamardon@yahoo.ca.

Printed in Canada by Golden Meteorite Press.

No part of this publication may be reproduced, stored in a retrieval system or transmitted, in any form or by any means, without prior written consent of the publisher or a licence from The Canadian Copyright Licensing Agency (Access Copyright). For an Access Copyright licence, visit: www.accesscopyright.ca or call toll free to 1-800-893-5777.

Supported by grant from Antarctic Institute of Canada.

Cover design Bianca Ho, 2012
Typeset by Bianca Ho, 2012
Published by Golden Meteorite Press.
126 Kingsway Garden
Post Office Box 34181
Edmonton, Alberta
T5G 3G4
Canada

Mardon, Austin A. (Austin Albert)
    The Liberals in power in Alberta, 1905-1921 / Austin Mardon, Ernest Mardon, G Zhou.

Includes bibliographical references.
ISBN 978-1-897480-08-3

    1. Liberal Party in Alberta--Biography. 2. Alberta--Politics and government--1905-1921. 3. Politicians--Alberta--Biography. I. Mardon, Ernest G., 1928- II. Zhou, G. (Gordon) III. Title.

FC3672.1.A1M373 2011   971.23'020922   C2011-905777-8

Dedicated to May Mardon

Contents

The Authors..8

Foreword...10

Preface..16

Introduction..17

The Lieutenant Governors....................................21

Chief Justices of Alberta.......................................22

The Senate..23

Senators from the Province of Alberta
 in Order of Appointment...................................24

Elective Representatives from Alberta.................25

The Early Years (1905-1921)................................26

Biographical Profiles...27

Index..87

Acknowledgements...93

The Authors

Ernest G. Mardon

Born December 21, 1928 at Houston, Texas, son of Professor Austin Mardon and his wife Marie Dickey. His father was of Devonshire yeoman stock. Educated at Gordonstown, Moray, Scotland and Cistercian College, Bosore, County Tripperary, Ireland, he attended Trinity College, Dublin University and Universita Italiana per Stranieri, Perugia. After being called up for National Service he saw active service as an officer with the Gordon Highlanders in the Middle East and Libya. Immigrating to Canada, he became a United States International staff correspondent and bureau manager in Winnipeg, Edmonton and Vancouver. After returning to the University to qualify as a teacher, he taught at Thibault High School, Morinville, Alberta. Later he received a Masters and Doctorate from the University of Ottawa. He has taught English Literature at five universities across the country.

Dr. Mardon is now retired, but continues his research on the Anglo Saxon Chronicle, and Alberta Politicians. In the summer he takes a break as a dishwasher at a Catholic Youth Camp near Red Deer. In 1957 he married May Knowler, an Edmonton teacher. They have one son, a daughter, and 3 grandsons.

Austin Albert Mardon

Born June 25, 1962, at Edmonton, son of Dr. Ernest G. Mardon and his wife May Knowler. Educated at Lethbridge, Mardon attended that University of Lethbridge. He has received a Masters of Science degree from South Dakota University and a Masters of Education degree from Texas A & M University. Mardon was a member of the 1986 NASA sponsored Antarctic meteorite recovery expedition. He is a member of the Explorer Club of New York.

Mardon's wide academic interests range from developing new methods for meteorite recovery to historical research of Alberta with his father. In 1991 he was elected to be a member of a Soviet Arctic expedition to Franz Joseph Land in the Soviet Arctic. Unfortunately, because of the domestic crisis in the Soviet Union, the project was cancelled after he arrived in Moscow.

He has authored over eighty scholarly communications and books.

Foreword

Statesmen From and For Alberta

Before proceeding with the political history and development of each constituency and short biographical sketches of those who functioned for the state and ruled us, which is the burden of this study, it would seem proper and necessary to present a sketch of the apparatus of state in which they functioned. In that way we may appreciate them and their contribution to our welfare all the more through understanding the function they performed and the power they wielded for us on behalf of the state they served.

Canada, since the passage of the British North America Act (BNA) by the Parliament of the United Kingdom and the Proclamation by Queen Victoria of July 1, 1867 as Confederation Day, is a federal state comprising two levels of constitutionally established government for the same Canadian citizen. There is a federal representative Parliament in Ottawa, comprised of the Crown, signified by the Governor General and appointed by the Crown on the advice of its Privy Council for Canada. The Governor General is effectively chosen by the federal cabinet, that is, the Senators and the Supreme Court Justices appointed by the Governor-General-in-Council, as well as the members of the House of Commons, elected by all Canadian citizens from specific geographically defined areas called federal ridings. Amongst the House of Commons is the Prime Minister and most of his Ministers, who constitute his Ministry of the federal Executive Council. On the other hand there is a provincial representative government in the capital of each of the now ten Canadian provinces, comprised of a Lieutenant-Governor who, with the justices of the superior courts of the province, is appointed by Ottawa, and the members elected periodically to the provincial Legislative Assembly by the residents of specific geographical constituencies. The province's constituencies have been divided and redivided as population warranted.

As Canada is a constitutional monarchy, a democracy but not a republic, there is again a division of function and authority at both the federal and provincial levels consisting of an amalgam of the Crown and the elected representatives. The Crown reigns while the elected members rule. Traditionally the Legislative and Executive branches of the State at both federal and provincial levels exist solely as advisors to the Crown in whom the ultimate authority of the State resides. Thus at the federal level we have a Governor-General appointed by the reigning Monarch by Letters Patent, which since 1947 transmit to him as representative practically all prerogatives of reign: the right to act as Head of State for Canada in all foreign or domestic relations and to be commander-in-chief of the Canadian Armed Forces. He receives ambassadors and proclaims war or peace, he has the right to grant Royal Pardon, the right to appoint Senators and Justices of the Supreme and Federal Counts as well as of superior courts in the provinces. He especially claims the right to call the leader of the majority political party returned at a general federal election to form a Cabinet, Executive Council, government of Ministry of which he will be the Prime Minister and to swear in the individual Ministers he has chosen to head the various Ministries of Departments of his government, as well as remove them. He has the duty to accept the resignation of a Prime Minister, whose ministry has lost majority support for his policies, especially those concerning financial matters in the House of Commons or whose maximum five year term of office has expired and issue writs for a general election whenever the Prime Minister requests it. He has the right, between general elections to open and close Sessions of Parliament and be available to the Prime Minister for constitution concerning the policy his Ministry will adopt and the legislation and enactment they will introduce to realize it. He encourages and warns him to sanction difficulties in the name of the Crown on behalf of the citizenry, and finally he has the right to sanction all Acts or legislation passed by Parliament or Orders, Writs, Proclamations or Appointments, etc. prepared by the Executive for his signature in order that thereby they will acquire the "force of law". He can never, never publicly propose any legislation or direction of policy himself or enter the political arena as the public protagonist of opinion of policies other than those espoused by Her Majesty's government and passed by Parliament.

  At the provincial level we have a simplified version of a similar arrangement between the Crown and the elected members. We have a Lieutenant Governor appointed by the Governor-General in Council for each province, whose functions are similar to those of the Governor-General at the federal except that he may withhold approval of doubtful provincial Legislation, Executive Orders, Proclamations, Writs Warrants, etc. until the Federal Executive will have had an opportunity to study them and their implications for the Nation. They may then either disallow them or refer them to the Supreme Court of Canada for a ruling on their validity or allow them to become law. The Federal can remove him from office, but once he has been appointed thereon, whereby he becomes the manifestation of the Crown in his own province and official Head of State there. He is no longer a local superintendent of provincial affairs for the Federal Executive that appointed him.

He too calls upon the leader of the party which won the last provincial general election, the premier, to form his governing Ministry or Cabinet. He swears them in as Ministers of the Executive Council, and appoints them as heads of Departments of Government. He opens and closes Session of the Legislative Assembly, sanctions all legislation passed there, as well as all proclamations, writs, warrants, etc. prepared by the Executive Council for his signature including those calling for a general election or a by-election. Even more so than his federal counterpart, must never state publicly or endorse any policy, legislation or enactment other than those of his government.

And so we see that at both levels, the federal and provincial the Crown reigns and the majority political party of elected members rules as Her Majesty's government and the minority party or parties as Her Majesty's equally loyal Opposition under a Prime Minister at the federal and a Premier at the provincial level. The Crown, above politics, becomes the principle and force for unity in the State at both levels, since debates in the House or the Assembly on policy, legislation or direction, based as they are on the "adversary principle" can become quite vehement and create disunity even divisiveness amongst those who in their totality are the real rulers in the sate; our elected representatives.

These members are generally elected on a political party basis by a majority vote of the residents of each particular riding for federal or constituency for provincial members on election day. Thereby the residents of that area are deemed to have endorsed the election platform of their candidate, which he or his party hammered out and adopted and which he and the other party spokesmen have presented to make supports of the residents and which he too is pledged to realize for them should he be selected.

These party platforms are intended to counteract flamboyant Public Relations and lower the amount of "impulse voting" which is based solely on a candidate's aura or charisma as manifested in personal or media appearances. "Impulse voting" can also be based exclusively on local issues or "gut" issues. Race, religion or language may also have bearing on a constituent's decision. Unfortunately on the present as in the past these issues usually win or lose the election even in this enlightened and electronic age, "Anything goes" to win a supporter on election day.

Political parties have an indispensable role to play at election time during actual governing. Without them, it would be difficult to ensure any sort of continuous policy for development at either level of government, to know who in fact won a general election and by virtue of party-solidarity of members after caucus discussion will ensure the government of majority support in the House or Assembly for its allotted five year span. Without political parties we would have a seriously reduced or indeed an entire "wipe-out" of supporters at the "grass roots" level, who now nominate candidate and contribute ideas, public relations and financial support for the ensuing campaign. Third parties tend to rely more heavily on the effective functioning of their local machinery, whereas the major parties generally duct them off only when a general election seems imminent. Third parties exist to ensure that a candidate will be chosen to sponsor an adaptation of the political party's known philosophy to the "here-and-now". They may not be constitutionally recognized, but are a necessary convention for the life and stability of representative democracy.

Both levels of government, the federal and provincial, each one sovereign and independent of the other in their exclusive areas of competence, are both concerned with the same citizen in the commonwealth, there can be conflict and there is certainly always tension in the pursuit of their objectives. In order that this tension might be minimized or at least remain controllable, the BNA Act has attempted to spill out the areas of competence or jurisdiction for each level. This it has done principally in Sections 91, 92, 93a, which are clarified by judicial decision or subsequent legislative addition of amendment. At the present point in time, discussion of areas of jurisdiction is confusing at best.

As guidelines, it might nevertheless be conceded that the provincial governments have been charged with ensuring the social well-being of their immediate constituency through enactments dealing primarily with "property and Civil right". The federal government, on the other hand, is charged with the "Nation's business". By virtue or Section 91, the federal is empowered to "make laws for Peace, Order and good Government in Canada for the nation as a unified whole, and in specified categories named in this Section as well as all areas not assigned by Section 92 to the exclusive jurisdiction of provincial governments. These named areas or categories are the exclusive responsibility of either level, except for the right to denominational schools which are governed by Magistrates or judges of their own provincial courts.

When Alberta became a province in 1905 the provincial government carried forward the court format that it had inherited from the Northwest Territories. The federal government confirmed in office for the province those who had been judges in the territorial courts there. Thus we had a Chief Justice of the Supreme Court of Alberta, divided into Trial and Appellate Divisions, and district courts for territorially determined areas whose presiding officers were known, not as justices, but as judges. Even those of provincial courts, although they were appointed by the Federal Government and with the Justices, who were also appointed, where to remain aloof from all political activity of any kind to the point of losing their voting franchise upon appointment to the Bench.

Above the provincial framework of courts was the Supreme Court of Canada constituted by statue and staffed by appointees of the federal government, who handled cases of both public and of private law, civil or criminal, either in the first instance or upon appeal from provincial or Court of Exchequer jurisdictions. The final and last Court of Appeal for Canadians was the Judicial Committee of the Privy Council in London.

When appeals to the Privy Council were abolished in 1949, criminal cases in 1933, the role of Court of Last Resort was passed back to the Supreme Court of civil cases in private law that it would hear. Ultimately it would seem destined to become principally the final interpreter of statues law from either federal or provincial levels or arbiters in conflicts between the two levels and final Court of Appeal for legitimated and accepted cases from provincial Supreme Courts. Hopefully this interpretation will not be to the extent that the Supreme Court in the U.S. is active in protecting the Constitutional Bill of Rights from being infringed upon by National or State Legislatures to the point of even determining ways and means by which these entrenched Right will be enhanced for the citizenry. Our Conventional Canadian view of Judges is that they must remain independent of politics in their decision. They must never enter into the political arena in any partisan way themselves in order to be better able to judge and interpret and apply laws or enactments made by the Legislative or Executive branches at both the federal and provincial levels dispassionately and justly ascending to the "rule of law" for the benefit of all.

Such then is a bird's eye view of our apparatus of state as it appears to the layman who is not a constitutional lawyer. The question of power or authority, its origin and exercise have always fascinated and intrigued me, this study of the proponent of power for the State in its three branches at its two levels. I have tried to write a short but pithy biography of each of these men in order that we might know more about them and their function. This study is of course only an initial first introduction of them to the reader and hopefully it will be follower by other researchers who will provide with more detailed biographies of at least the more outstanding leaders amongst them. Nevertheless, it is hoped that the beginnings we have gathered here will provide the reader with a nearer look at the men and women who filled these roles of power for the State and for the common good of us all: Canadians and Albertans.

Tremblay

Preface

The following compendium of biographies covers those participants on the Alberta political scene during the first decade and a half of the existence of the Province of Alberta from 1905-1921. These following persons were the men and women who established our political institutions in the age of the Pioneer.

The aim of this work is to cover all politicians; both at the federal and provincial levels, during the formative years while the Liberals controlled the Legislature. Biographical sketches include federally appointed Alberta Senators and Lieutenant Governors, elected members of Parliament from Alberta Ridings and elected members of the Alberta Legislature and unsuccessful candidates.

The result is a condensed biographical entry from each one. The reader who is interested in election statistics and data are referred to *Alberta Election Results 1882-1992* compiled by the same authors and published for Alberta Community Development. (1993).

A variety of sources were consulted. All facts and dates were checked and verified from written published material that was extracted from newspapers, daily and weekly of the period, and other accessible documents.

These specific biographical profiles have been excerpted from a much larger opus still in preparation. We apologize for the brevity of some candidates' summaries herein, but hope that this failing will be connected by ongoing research. Public documents and published material were, of course, basic to this archival study, as were all accessible sources of information, including interviews with living descendants. The Macleod Gazette, The Edmonton Bulletin, the Calgary Albertan, the Edmonton Journal, the Calgary Herald, the Lethbridge Herald, the Camrose Canadian, and the Coronation Review were of great assistance in providing source material.

It was only by writing the biographies of all candidates tat it was possible to find out about kinship networks, business networks and legal networks and important contribution made by those persons whose names appear in this work are the Founding Fathers of the Province of Alberta.

E.G.M. & A.A.M.

Introduction

This collection of biographies is derived from the earlier pages of Alberta's illustrious history. The biographies are rooted in the pioneer period; they are sketches of those who laid the province's political foundations. In a way, this work is comparable to Hesiod's Theogony, as it presents the birth of the province through the lens of a handful of key individuals. These individuals' contributions continue to reverberate through the province's history just as the Titans and Olympians outlined in the Theogony explained the universe to centuries of Greeks and inspired further myths. That is not to say that the members of Alberta's first government are gods but that they outlined the manner in which future governments would behave. The structure of government explained in the essay by Trembley presented earlier in this book would have been first proposed by these early government officials, a structure that remains firmly intact today. Beyond the significance of the time period, the work offers another inkling of how the province got to be the way it is. It provides biographical profiles not only on the few lucky individuals who managed to obtain office, whether that be in the Alberta legislature or the Canadian parliament, but also on the many who tried and failed to be elected. Though one may not be elected, his adversary must still be sensitive to his position. A successful candidate's triumph must come by making his argument distinct from others or he must make his position more flexible to counteract possible criticism from his competitors. Regardless, simply by running for office an individual still manages to affect change and stimulate a reaction. In addition, by presenting those who 'lose' elections alongside those who 'win' them, it becomes easier to assess the overall sentiment of the time period. The work makes itself susceptible to these possibilities of interpretation as each entry is crafted objectively. Analysis is the reader's responsibility. The lack of personal bias allows these biographical entries to be used for research or even as fodder for storytellers. By delineating in those early years all involved in electoral races and by maintaining an objective stance, the work provides a fertile seedbed for theories involving both the history of the province as well as its current state of affairs. As editor, I have endeavored to enhance the accessibility of the work so that it may be easily included in other examinations of Alberta.

Claire MacMaster

The Lieutenant-Governors

The Lieutenant-Governor is both the representative of the federal government in the Canadian provinces, appointed, instructed and dismissible by it, and the representative of the monarchy insofar as the working of cabinet government is concerned. Since these two aspects are so completely fused in one office, it is often impossible to clearly separate them and the discretionary powers of the representative of the monarchy may on occasion be used in the interest of the federal government.

Moreover, since the federal government is formed from a political party, it is often difficult to separate the interests of the government from the interests of the party. The province of Alberta and her neighboring prairie province of Saskatchewan were created by an act of the federal government in 1905.

Liberal Prime Minister Wilfred Laurier named the first Lieutenant-Governor of Alberta. He was George Bulyea, a forty-six year old former cabinet minister in the Haultain administration of the Northwest Territories. He had Liberal affiliations. Bulyea was appointed to a second five-year term in 1910.

The second Lieutenant-Governor was Dr. Robert Brett of Banff. Conservative Prime Minister Robert Borden named him to the position in 1915. He had sat in the Northwest Territories legislature in Regina as the leader of the opposition. He later served as the president of the Alberta Conservative Association.

The Chief Justices of Alberta

At times when the Lieutenant-Governor cannot fulfill his duties, the Chief Justice of the Appellate Division of the Supreme Court of Alberta takes over. They are therefore included in this work.

List of Chief Justices of Alberta – 1905-1972

Arthur Sifton   1905-1910
Horace Harvey 1910-1921
David L. Scott   1921-1924
Horace Harvey 1924-1949

The Senate

While the Senate possesses legal power almost equal to that of the House of Commons, and is in theory an independent legislative body, it is in actual practice a minor partner in the legislature. Three constitutional principles emphasize this fact, the first two explicit, and the third unwritten. These three principles are that: only the House of Commons is based on popular election, the House of Commons has the sole power to originate money bills, and the cabinet is responsible to the House of Commons and not to the Senate.

The main functions and duties of the Senate are to act as a revising and restraining body and to protect the interest of the provinces and minority racial, religious and language groups.

The first great handicap which was placed on the Senate at Confederation was the system under which its members were appointed. With only a few notable exceptions, appointments to the Red Chamber have been made by the Prime Minister of the day to faithful party supporters. Goldwin Smith states. "The Senate is a bribery fund in the hands of the government, and paddock for the 'Old War Horse' of the party, nor, on its present footing, will it ever by anything else;...a minister cannot help himself; the goods in the shape of party services and expenditures on elections have been delivered, and he is compelled to pay."

Under the Alberta Act of 1905, Alberta was to have four Senators. This number was increased to six in 1915.

Senators From the Province of Alberta In Order of Appointment

According to the Alberta Act which created the province in 1905, the newly-created province had the right to have four Senators.

James Lougheed, of Calgary, Conservative (1888-1925)
Phillippe Roy, of Edmonton, Liberal (1906-1911)
Peter Talbot, of Lacombe, former Liberal MP for Alberta (1906-1919)
Dr. L. George De Veber, of Lethbridge, former Liberal MLA (1906-1925)
Amedee Forget, of Banff, Liberal (1911-1923)

The number of Senators from Alberta was increased to six in 1915

Edward Michener, of Red Deer, former Conservative MLA (1918-1948)
W.J. Harmer, of Edmonton (1918-1948)

Elective Representatives From Alberta

The House of Commons

The House of Commons is the real centre of parliamentary authority and exercises a preponderant influence in the government. It is the organized medium through which the public finds expression and exercises its ultimate political power. It forms the indispensable part of the legislature and it is the body to which the executive must turn for justification and approval. It is based on popular election and, basically province, with provision for adjustment after each decennial census.

There has been a total of one hundred and twenty members of Parliament elected since 1905 to represent the province in Ottawa: forty six Conservatives, thirty four Liberal, twenty eight Social Creditors (two of them crossing party lines – one to join the Conservatives [Robert Thompson of Red Deer] and the other the Liberal [Bud Olson of Medicine Hat]) and fourteen United Farmers of Alberta. Douglas Harkness, P.C., has represented Calgary in Ottawa for a longer period of time than any other M.P. – a total of twenty-seven years.

The number of ridings in the province has increased from four in 1904 to nineteen as of the last federal election in 1968.

The Early Years (1905-1921)

When Alberta was created by act of Parliament, it was sending four members to Ottawa: two Conservatives and two Liberals. In 1908 the province's representation was increased to seven: three were Conservatives and four were Liberals. In the 1911 general election that saw Robert Borden and the Conservatives take power for the first time in fifteen years, Alberta did not go with the rest of Canada. It sent six Liberals to Ottawa, and the only Conservative was R.B. Bennet, the Calgary lawyer who was to become the Prime Minister of Canada some twenty years later.

Biographical Profiles

Frederick W. Archer

Born September 7, 1872 at Campbellford, Ontario, son of Charles P. Archer and his wife Maria. He was of ethnic English descent and an Anglican. He was educated in Ontario and qualified as an accountant. As a young man he saw active service with Colonel Boulton's Montreal Militia unit in the Northwest Rebellion of W.R. Brock Company at Montreal from 1895 to 1906. Coming to Alberta he served as the manager of the Calgary branch of the W.R. Brock firm or four years. Archer then became a prominent Calgary real estate and insurance agent. Frederick W. Archer was returned the Liberal member in 1913. He sat as a private member on the government side of the chamber for four years. In 1917 he did not seek re-election but retired from politics at the age of forty-five.

[See: Who's Who and Why, (1913)]

Henry P. Atkins

Born July 3, 1867 in Yorkshire, England, son of Henry Burns Atkins and his wife Jane Wilson. He was a Protestant and a freemason. Educated at the City York College, he then became a rancher. By 1906 he owned the first Didsbury elevator and was a successful businessman. He also was a farm implement deal. He served as the mayor of Didsbury. Henry P. Atkins was returned as the Liberal member for Didsbury in 1917. He sat in the Legislature for four years as a government backbencher. In 1921 he did not seek re-elections but retired from politics at the age of fifty-four.

George Russell Barker

Born October 26, 1881 at Melbourne, Australia, son of Col. John Barker and Christina Leslie. He was of Scottish descent and an Anglican. His father was a military officer in charge of the Melbourne Royal Mint. Younger Barker's grandfather was the proprietor of a large sheep ranch in the State of Victoria, Australia. He returned to English to attend Bradfield College, Berkshire and later served as a British and Indian army officer in the artillery. After leaving the army in 1904, he came to Canada and became a landowner in the Lac St. Anne district. He was an unsuccessful candidate in the 1913 general election. Russell Barker was returned as the Conservative member for Lac St. Anne in 1917. He sat in the Legislature for four years as a member of the opposition. It was said at the time that he was the owner of the largest house between Edmonton and Dawson City, Yukon. In 1921 he did not seek re-election but retired from politics.

[See: Canadian Parliamentary Guide, (1921)]

Richard Bedford Bennett

Born July 3 1870 at Hopewell Hill, New Brunswick, son of Henry John Bennett and his wife Henrietta Styles. His father was a ship builder. He was of ethnic English descent of United Empire Loyalist stock and a Methodist. Educated at the Provincial Normal School and taught for a couple years. He attended Dalhousie University and graduated in law. He was admitted to the New Brunswick bar and joined the Leumal J. Tweedie Chathain legal firm. He stayed in Chathain for four years. Coming to the Northwest Territories, he settled at Calgary where he became a partner of Senator James A. Lougheed in 1891. He also was the solicitor of the Canadian Pacific Railway. Richard B. Bennett was returned the member for Calgary West in 1898. He sat in the NWT assembly for seven years. In 1905 he was defeated in the first Alberta general election. Bennett was named the Alberta Conservative leader and returned as one of the two Calgary members in 1909. He became the leader of the Opposition. He sat in the Legislature for two stormy years during the railway scandal debate, the resignation of Premier Rutherford and the appointment by Lt. Governor Bulyea of Chief Justice of Alberta, Arthurs L. Sifton as the Premier. In 1911 Bennett vacated his seat to enter federal politics. Bennett was returned as the Conservative member for the Calgary West riding in 1911. He sat for a total of nineteen years in the House of Commons, from 1911 to 1917 and from 1935 to 1938. For the last five, he was the Prime Minister. He did not seek re-election in 1917 and was defeated in his bid to re-enter the Commons in 1921. In the 1929 Winnipeg Convention he was selected the National leader of the Conservative party. In 1935 he became the leader of the Opposition. In 1938, he vacated his seat and retired form politics. The next year he moved to the United Kingdom where he purchased the large estate of Michele home, Surrey. In 1941 King George VI created him Viscount Bennet of Michleham, Calgary and Hopewell and he took his seat in House of Lords. He died June 27, 1947 at Dorking, England.

[See: Canadian Who's Who, (1938)]

William John Blair

Born October 13, 1875 at Embro, Ontario, son of John Blair and his wife Ellen Smyth. He was of Anglo-Irish descent and an Anglican. Educated at Woodstock, he attended the Toronto School of Practical Science graduated as a mining engineer. He came to Alberta in 1906 and homesteaded in the Provost district. Later he became a prominent farmer in the area. He was an unsuccessful provincial candidate in the 1913 election. William J. Blair was returned as the Unionist Pro-government member for the Battle River riding in 1917. He sat in the House of Commons for four years.

[See: Canadian Parliamentary Guide, (1918)]

Dr. Thomas Henry Blow

Born January 22, 1862 at South Mountain, Ontario, son of Robert H. Blow and his wife Sarah Henderson. His father was a carriage manufacturer of Dunchas. He was of ethnic Scottish descent and a Presbyterian. He also was a high-ranking Freemason. Educated at Kempville, he attended McGill University graduating in medicine in 1895. He became a South Mountain physician. Later he took specialist training at Edinburgh University. He became an eye, ear, nose and throat specialist. He worked for a year as a specialist at Denver, Colorado. Came to the Northwest Territories in 1903, he settled at Calgary where he practiced his profession for the next thirty years. He failed to establish a University at Calgary. He was an unsuccessful candidate in 1909. Dr. Thomas H. Blow was returned as the Conservative member for Calgary South in 1913. He sat in the Legislature for eight years as an Opposition member. In 1921 he was defeated and retired from politics at the age of fifty-nine. He died December 27th, 1932 at Vancouver.

[See: Who's Who and Why, (1912)]

Lucien Boudreau

Born August 17, 1877 at St. Gregoire, Quebec, son of Dr. J.B.A. Boudreau and his wife. He was of ethnic French Canadian descent and a Roman Catholic. His ancestors came to New France in the 17th century. His brother Rudolphe Beaudreau served for twenty four years to Wildred Laurier before he became clerk of the Privy Council in 1896. He was educated at St. Gregoire. He came to the Northwest Territories in 1900 and settled at St. Albert where he became the proprietor of a hotel. He was a large lumber merchant. He served as the Mayor of St. Albert for five years. He was an unsuccessful candidate in 1905. Lucien Beaudreau was returned the Liberal member for St. Albert in 1909. He was an unsuccessful candidate in 1930 and again in 1935. Lucien Beaudreau is remembered as the only member of the Legislature who voted against the bill granting female suffrage in 1916. He died December 19, 1962. He was a brother in law of Omer Germained, M.L.A. (1930-1935)

[See: Who's Who and Why, (1912)]

John Robert Boyle, K.C.

Born February 3. 1871 in Lounlton County, Ontario, son of William Boyle and his wife Anne E. McClean. He was of ethnic Scottish descent and a Presbyterian. He was also a Freemason. He came to the Northwest Territories in 1894, and settled at Regina where he attended the Normal School and qualified as a teacher. He taught there for some time. Moving to Edmonton, Boyle studied law under Hedley C. Taylor (later Judge Taylor). After bring admitted to the N.W.T. Bar in

1899, he joined the legal partnership of Taylor, Boyle, and Parlee. He served as an alderman in 1904. John R. Boyle was returned the Liberal member for Sturgeon in 1905. He sat in the Legislature for eighteen years. He served as the Deputy Speaker in 1906. During the railway scandal of 1910, he bitterly attacked premier Rutherford and was one of the leading "Liberal insurgents". Premier Sifton appointed him to the Cabinet as the Minister of Education in 1913. Five years later Premier Stewart named Boyle the Attorney General in 1918. He held this port for three years. In 1922 he was named the Leader of the Opposition. In 1924 he vacated his seat on being appointed a Justice of the Alberta Supreme Court: Trial Division. Justice Boyle died while still on the Bench February 15, 1936 at Ottawa from bronchial pneumonia while on his way to Bermuda. He was sixty-five years of age.

[See: Who's Who and Why, (1912)]

Alwyn Bramley-Moore

Born in 1878 at London, England, song of the Rev. W. Bramley-Moore and his wife. He was of ethnic English descent and an Anglican. He came to Ontario in 1895 and to Alberta in 1904 as a Barr Colonist where he homesteaded near Lloydminster. Alwyn Bramley-Moore was returned as the Liberal member for Alexandra (Lloydminster) in 1909. He sat in the Legislature as a vocal government backbencher. In 1913 he id not seek re-election and retired from politics. He became well-known after the publication of Canada and Her Colonies or Home Rule for Alberta (1911). The book dealt extensively with such longstanding issues such as the relationship between the provinces and the federal government and the ownership of natural resources. He took up the cause of Alberta against what he called "Eastern Tyranny" and defined what he saw as "conflicting interests of the east and west". One of this statements could be said to reflect the philosophy of many of the Canadian provinces today: "The true principle that must be embodied in any constitution undertaking to hold together an aggregate of national units, be they racial or geographical, the true principle is the fullest autonomy for the separate units." Indeed, Bramley-Moore went so far as to advocate eventual secession, but only as a mechanism to enhance Alberta's bargaining position vis-à-vis the federal government. A thought worthy of any sustained while on active service at Vimy Ridge in April, 1916.

[See: Canadian Parliamentary Guide, (1913)]

W. Fletcher Bredin

Born in 1857 at Glengarry, Ontario, son of a farmer. He was of Anglo-Irish descent and an Anglican. He came to Manitoba as a young man in 1877 to farm near Winnipeg. Later he travelled widely across North America. While on a trip down the Athabasca River, he met Rev. Thomas Marsh, an Anglican missionary and later married Mash's sister Ann of Hay River. He explored the Mackenzie River to the Arctic Ocean, and finally settled on a homestead near Grouard. W. Fletcher Bredin was returned as the Liberal member by acclamation for Athabasca constituency in 1905. He sat in the Legislature for four years as a government backbencher. In 1909 he was defeated by fellow Liberal Jean-Leon Cote and retired from politics.
[See: Who's Who and Why, (1912)]

Thomas "Allie" Brick"

Born January 2, 1857 at Compton, Quebec, son of John G. Brick and his wife Emma Marie Brick. He was of ethnic English descent and a Methodist. He was educated at Toronto. He came to Northwest Territories as a young man, he settles at Peace River Crossing where he operated a ferry and became a successful Grouard farmer. T. "Allie" Brick was returned the Liberal member for Peace River in the February 4, 1906 by-election. He sat in the Legislature for three years as a government backbencher. In 1909 he did not seek re-election but retired form politics. He died in 1942.

[See: Canadian Parliamentary Guide, (1952)]

William Asbury Buchanan

Born July 2,1876 at Fraserville, Ontario, son of William Buchanan, a Methodist minister, and his wife Mary Pentine. He was of ethnic Scottish descent and a strong Methodist. Educated at Norwood, Ontario, he became a journalist with the Peterborough Review from 1893 to 1898, and The Toronto Telegram from 1898 to 1903. He came to the Northwest Territories and he settled at Lethbridge where he founded the Lethbridge Herald in 1905. He was the publisher of the ministral daily newspaper for forty-nine years. William A. Buchanan was returned was the Liberal member for Lethbridge in 1909. Premier Rutherford immediately took him into the Cabinet as a Minister without Portfolio. A year later he resigned from the Cabinet over the railway scandal. He then vacated his seat to enter federal politics. William A. Buchanan was Pro-Borden government member in Lethbridge in 1917. He sat in the House of Commons for ten years. In 1931 he did not seek re-election. Buchanan was summoned to the Senate September 5 1925. He died July 11, 1954 at Lethbridge.

[See: Canadian Who's Who, (1952)]

George Hedley Vicars Bulyea

Born February 17, 1857 at Gagetown, N.B., son of James A. Bulyea and his wife Jane Blizzard. On both sides he was of United Empire Loyalist stock. He was of ethnic English descent and a Baptist. Educated at Gagetown, he attended the University of New Brunswick graduating in arts in 1878. He served as the registrar for Queen's merchant and fungeral parlor director. He was an unsuccessful candidate in 1891. G.H.V. Bulyea was returned as the member for South Qu'Appelle in 1892. He sat in the N.W.T. assembly for eleven years. He served as Minister of Agriculture and Commissioner of Public Works. Prime Minister Laurier named G.H.V. Bulyea as Alberta's first Lieutenant Governor, He held this position for ten years. In 1915 he retired form public life at the age of fifty-eight.

[See: Who's Who and Why, (1912)]

Archibald Campbell

Born in 1862. He was of ethnic Scottish descent and a Presbyterian. He became an Innis free farmer. Archie Campbell was returned the Liberal member for Vermillion in 1909. He sat in the Legislature for a year as a government backbencher. In June 1910, he vacated his seat to permit the new premier, former Chief Justice Arthur L. Sifton to enter the Chamber.

[See: Canadian Parliamentary Guide, (1911)]

Robert Eldo Campbell

Born August 15, 1871 in Lanark Country, Ontario, son of John Campbell and his wife Jane Roe. He was of Anglo-Irish descent and a Methodist. Educated at Barrie, he cam to the Northwest Territories as a young man. He attended the Regina Normal School graduated as a teacher. He taught at Banff before becoming a mountain guide for the Canadian Pacific Railway. He organized and as a charter member of the Canadian Alpine club. He spent twenty years in the Rocky Mountains. He then moved to Calgary where he became a grain dealer. Robert E. Campbell was returned the Conservative member of the Rocky Mountain constituency in 1913. He sat in the Legislature as an opposition member for eight years. At the outbreak of World War I, he enlisted in the Canadian Army and proceeded overseas as a captain of the 191st Battalion. He saw active service on the Western Front. In 1921 he was defeated by Liberal Dr. J.E. State in the Clearwater Constituency. He died October 1956 at a Vancouver Western Conference Football Final game of the season.

[See: Canadian Parliamentary Guide, (1921)]

Dr. William Alexander Campbell

Born March 31, 1873 at Nairn, Middlesex County, Ontario, son of James M. Campbell and his wife Isabella Campbell. His father was the storekeeper at Toronto's prison. He was of ethnic Scottish descent and a Presbyterian. Educated at Stathroy, he attended the University of Toronto, graduating in medicine. Came to the Northwest Territories as a young man, he settled at Ponoka where he was a physician and a coroner. Dr. William A. Campbell was returned as the Liberal member for Ponoka in 1909. He sat in the Legislature for eight years. In 1917 he was defeated by Conservative Charles O. Cunningham and retired from politics at the age of forty-four. He died in 1934.

[See: Canadian Parliamentary Guide, (1917)]

Michael Clark, W.B., C.M.

Born in 1861 at Belford, Northumberland, England. His father was an Englishman and his mother was of Scottish descent. He never indicated his religious affiliation. He was born into a wealthy family. Educated at Elmfield College, he attended Edinburgh University. He graduated with two medical degrees. Dr. Clark became a Newcastle-Upon-Tyne physician for twenty years. When he arrived in Canada, he settled near Olds, Alberta, NWT, he was the proprietor of the large Belford ranch. After coming here he never practiced medicine. He was an unsuccessful Liberal candidate in 1905. Dr. Michael Clark was returned the Liberal member for the Red Deer riding in 1908. He sat in the House of Commons for thirteen years. In 1917 he cross the floor of the Commons to join the Unionist Pro-Borden government party. He again crossed the floor of the Commons to sit as a "Progressive"-farmer member in 1920. In 1921 he was unsuccessful as a Liberal in Mackenzie riding. He then retired to his ranch at the age of sixty. He died July 26, 1926 at Olds. Dr. Clark, a brilliant public speaker, as always referred to as "Red Michael"- not for his views but because he represented the Red Deer riding.

[See: Who's Who and Why, (1910)]

James K. "Peace River Jim" Cornwall

Born October 29, 1869 at Brantford, Ontario son of Thomas Cornwall and Hannah Kennedy. He was Educated at Brantford. He left home at the age of fourteen to sell newspapers on the streets of Buffalo, New York. He was a sailor on a lumber freighter, sailing out of New York for many years. He came to the district of Alberta, N.W.T. in 1896, he worked on railway construction, he established himself. Later he worked at Athabasca Landing, trading with the Indians and trapping for furs. He assisted Klondike Gold Rushers to navigate the danger of rapids on the Athabasca River. He charged $25.00 a person to piloting boats safely through the rapids. He and Fletcher Bredin were associated with "Alli Brick" Davis in opening up the Peace River country for homesteaders. Interest in provincial politics J.K. Cornwall entered politics in the 1906 Peace River by-election when he ran successfully as one of the two Liberal Candidates in the Pace River constituency. Four years later Cornwall was returned to the Legislature by acclamation. He sat until he retired in 1913. While in the Legislature, he pressed the government to build railway lines into the Peace River country and to Athabasca Landing. His efforts were successful. Upon the outbreak of World War I he entered the Canadian Army and saw active service on the Western Front with the 8th Battalion. He was awarded the D.S.O. Colonel Cornwall unsuccessfully contested the "Overseas Soldiers" constituency. On his return to Canada he continued his trading and exploring activities in the northland. In the 1921 Alberta Election, Cornwall unsuccessfully contested the multi-member Edmonton constituency as an Independent. In a field of twenty-six candidates he placed sixteenth. He died November 20, 1955 at the age of eighty-five.

[See: Canadian Who's Who, (1936)]

Herbert Howard Crawford

Born March 10, 1878 at Brampton, Ontario, son of Robert Crawford and his wife Amelia James. He was of ethnic Scottish descent and a Methodist. He was educated at Brampton. He became a land surveyor. He came to the Northwest Territories as a young man, settling at Edmonton where he became a prominent merchant, auctioneer and manufacturer. He was member of Strathcona's first town council. Herbert W. sat in the Legislature for eight years as a member of the opposition. In 1921, he was defeated in his re-election bid. He died in 1924 at Calgary.

[See: Canadian Parliamentary Guide, (1921)]

Charles Wilson Cross, K.C.

Born November 30, 1872 at Madoc, Ontario, son of Thomas Cross and his wife Marie Mouncey. He was born into a wealthy family. He was of ethnic Scottish descent and a Presbyterian. Educated at Upper Canada College, he attended the University of Toronto, graduating in arts, and Toronto's Osgoode Hall Law School. He was admitted to the Ontario Bar in 1898. Coming to the Northwest Territories, he settled at Edmonton where he became a prominent lawyer. Charles W. Cross was appointed by Premier Rutherford the Attorney General of the new province of Alberta in September 1905. He was returned to the Legislature for Edmonton in the November 9th election. He sat in the Legislature for twenty years, then as the Attorney General. From 1913 to 1917 he represented two constituencies in the Legislature, Edmonton and Edson. In 1925 he vacated his seat to enter federal politics. He died June 2, 1928 at Calgary. In 1900 he had married Anne L. Lynde. They had one son, Thomas Lynde Cross (1900-1977) who became a Northern Alberta District Court Judge.

[See: Alberta Past and Present, (1924)]

Charles O. Cunningham

He was a Ponoka farmer. Charles O. Cunningham returned as the Conservative member for Ponoka in 1917. He sat in the Legislature for four years as an Opposition member. In 1921 he was defeated by UFA candidate Percival Baker and retired from politics. He died in 1942 at Ponoka.

[See: Canadian Parliamentary Guide, (1921)]

William Henry Cushing

Born August 21, 1852 in Wellington County, Canada West, son of William Cushing and his wife Sarah Thompson. His father was a successful farmer. He was of ethnic English descent and a Methodist. Young Cushing was a farmer from 1865 – 1879 in Willington County. He then became a building contractor. When came to the Northwest Territories, he settled at Calgary where he became a prominent lumber merchant and manufacturer of doors and window frames. He served a Calgary alderman from 1890 to 1906. William H. Cushing was appointed to premier Rutherford's first cabinet as Minister of Public Works in September 1905. He was returned as the member for Calgary in the first general election. He sat in the Legislature for eight years. In 1910 when Premier Rutherford resigned because of a railway scandal, it was expected that Lt. Governor Bulyea would ask Cushing to form a government. This did not happen. Cushing then sat as an Independent Liberal. In 1913 he did not seek re-election but retired from politics at the age of sixty. He died in 1934.

[See: MacRae. The History of Alberta, (1912)]

William McCartney Davidson, B.A.

Born November 12, 1872 at Hillie, Ontario, son of James C. Davidson and his wife Sarah. He was of Anglo-Irish/United Empire Loyalist descent and a Presbyterian. Educated at Picton and St. Catherine, he attended the University of Toronto, graduating in arts. From 1894 to 1901 he was a reporter with "The Toronto Star". He Came to the Northwest Territories and settled at Calgary where he became the founder and published of the Calgary Albertan in 1902. William M. Davidson was returned as the Liberal member for Calgary North in 1917. He spent a total of six years in the Legislature. First from 1917 to 1921, before he was defeated in the general election. He re-entered the Legislature by returned a Liberal member in January 15, 1923 by-election. The vacancy had been caused by the death of R.C. Edwards, the publisher of the Calgary Eye Opener. Davidson vacated his seat to enter federal politics in 1925. He was defeated in his attempt to win the Calgary East riding in the October 29, 1925 federal election by Conservative Fred Davis. Davidson then retired from politics at the age of fifty-three. He died in 1942 at Calgary.

[See: Canadian Parliamentary Guide, (1925)]

Frederick Davis

Born March 26, 1868 at Mitchell, Ontario, son of W.R. Davis and his wife I.L. Worth. His father was the publisher and managing editor of "The Mitchell Advocate" for fifty-eight years. He was of ethnic English descent and a Protestant. While a young man he served the Mayor of Mitchell. He came to the Northwest Territories, he settles at Calgary. Later he became a famer and the proprietor of a knitting factory. Fred Davis was returned as an Independent member for Gleichen in 1917. He sat in the Legislature for four years as an Opposition member. In 1921 he did not seek re-election. Turning to federal politics, Davis was returned the Independent member for the Calgary East riding in 1925. He sat in the House of Commons for one year. In 1926 he was defeated by Liberal H.B. Adshead and retired from politics at the age of fifty-eight. His date of death is unknown.

James McCrie Douglas

Born February 5, 1867 at Middleville, Lanark County, Canada West, son of James Douglas, a Presbyterian minister, and his wife Margaret Blyth. He was of ethnic Scottish descent and a strong Presbyterian. He came to Canada as a young child and was educated at Morris, Manitoba. In 1894 he married May Cameron Bickerton of Glasgow. They had no children. He came to Strathcona, South Edmonton in 1894, he and his brother Robert Blyth Douglas became prominent merchants in the firm of Douglas Brothers. James M. Douglas was returned the Liberal member for the Strathcona riding in the October 20, 1909 by-election to fill the vacancy caused by the death of the sitting member Dr. Wilbert McIntyre. He sat in the House of Commons for twelve years. In 1917 he crossed the floor of the Commons, abandoning the Laurier Liberals to join the Union Pro-Borden government. In 1921, Douglas running as a Conservative candidate, was defeated by the UFA member Daniel Webster Warner in his re-election bid. There was no record of his death found.

[See: MacRae. The History of Alberta, (1912)]

Dr. Leverett George De Veber

Born February 10, 1849 at St. John, New Brunswick, son of Richard Sandys DeVeber and his wife Caroline Beer, the daughter of a British naval captain. He was of English descent and an Anglican. His great-grandfather, Col. Gabriel De Veber had served in the British army during the rebellion of the American colonies. After the war he moved north to New Brunswick. George De Veber was educated at Windsor, Nova Scotia Bartholomew Hospital, London England, and then University of Pennsylvania, graduating in medicine. He practiced his profession in Lethbridge. George De Veber was elected as the Liberal member for Lethbridge in the Northwest Territorial Council in the general elections of 1898 and 1902. He served as the government whip in the Assembly. Upon the creation of the Province of Alberta he entered the cabinet as a Minister Without Portfolio, but resigned on being summoned to the Senate March 6, 1906. Senator DeVeber died July 9, 1925.

[See: Alberta Past and Present, (1924)]

Robert Barry Eaton

Born August 5, 1871 at Truro, Nova Scotia, son of James K. Eaton, Canadian Engineer, and A.K. Petblado. He was of English descent and an Anglican. He was educated at Truro. During the South African war, he served with the Southern Constabulary and remained with it after the war. As a young man he came to the Northwest Territories and homesteaded in Craigmyle district in 1904. He became a well-known famer. He also operated a farm fox. Robert B. Eaton was returned as the Liberal member for Hand Hills in 1913. He sat in the Chamber as a government backbencher for eight years. In 1921 he was defeated in the bid for re-election by UFA candidate George Foster and retired from politics at the age of fifty. During World War II he served overseas seeing active service on the Western Front. He rose to the rank of Colonel. In 1935 Eaton retired in Chillowack, B.C.

[see: Canadian Parliamentary Guide, (1921)]

Arthur Wellesley Ebbett, K.C.

Born January 3, 1866 at Hampstead, N.B. son of Charles H. Ebbett and his wife Elizabeth M. Penny. He was of ethnic English descent and a Baptist. His great grandfather, Arthur W. Ebbett, had left the New England colonies after the Revolutionary Wars in the 1780's. He attended the University of New Brunswick graduating in 1889, and was admitted to the New Brunswick Bar in 1890. In 1892 he was appointed a Queen's County judge. He left the Bench in 1896. Upon arriving in Alberta he became a Mannville lawyer. Arthur W. Ebbett was returned as the Liberal member for Vermillion in the October, 1917 be-election by acclamation. He sat in the Legislature for almost four years as a government backbencher. 1921 he was defeated by UFA candidate Richard Gavin Reid and retired from politics at the age of fifty-five. He was an unsuccessful provincial candidate in 1926.

[See: Alberta: Past and Present, (1924)]

Albert Freeman Ewing, K.C.

Born June 29, 1871 at Elora, Ontario son of Alexander Ewin and his wife Mary Monarey. He was of Ulster Scott descent of United Empire Loyalist stock and a Presbyterian. He attended the University of Toronto graduating in Arts. He was admitted to the Ontario Bar. Coming to the Northwest Territories, he settled at Edmonton where he became a prominent lawyer. He was an unsuccessful candidate in 1909. Albert F. Ewing was returned as the Conservative member for Edmonton in 1913. He sat in the Legislature for eight years one of which as the Leader of the Opposition. In 1921 he was defeated. He was an unsuccessful candidate in the 1923 by-election. Justice Minister Hugh Guthrie appointed Ewing to the Alberta Supreme Court: Trial Division in 1931. Ten Years later he was elevated to the Appellate Division. He was the first Chairman of the Farmer's Creditors' Arrangement Act Board, and held that post until 1935, when he was succeeded by Chief Justice C.R. Mitchell. Mr. Justice Ewing served on the Commission appointed to investigate the Nordegg Mine disaster, which cost the lives of more than 100 miners. His report was considered a masterpiece in thoroughness and clarity. In 1904 he married the former Jean Lafferty, of Perth, Ontario, who died in 1933. In 1935 he married the former Jean McFarquhar of Thorby, Alberta. He was a Presbyterian. He died August 28, 1946 at Edmonton at the age of 75. A week before he died, Mr. Justice Ewing had tendered his resignation from the Bench to Justice Minister Louis St. Laurent.

[See: Canadian Who's Who, (1936)]

William Thomas Finlay

Born July 12, 1863 at Lisburg, Ireland, son of John Finlay and his wife Christina. He was of ethnic Ulster Scott decent and a Presbyterian. He was educated at Belfast's Royal Academy. He came to Canada as a young man and settled at Medicine Hat, Assiniboine West. He claimed to be the first resident in 1883. He became a powerful lumber merchant. He served as the mayor of Medicine Hat from 1900 to 1902. He also had ranching interests. William T. Finlay was returned the member for Medicine Hat in 1902. He sat in the N.W.T. Assembly for three years. In September 1905, premier Rutherford took Finlay into the Cabinet as the Minister of Agriculture and Provincial Secretary. He was in failing health. After Premier Rutherford resigned, Finlay vacated his seat so that former judge C.R. Mitchell could enter the chamber after he had been sworn in as Attorney General and Minister of Education. William T. Finlay died May 14, 1914 at Vancouver.

[See: MacRae. The History of Alberta, (1912)]

Charles Wellington Fisher

Born August 4, 1866 at Hyde Park, London, England, song of James Fisher and his wife Elizabeth. He was born into a wealthy family. He was of ethnic English descent and a Presbyterian. Coming to the Northwest Territories he settled at Cochrane where he became the most prominent merchant. Charles W. Fisher was returned as the member for Banff in 1902 and sat in the NWT Assembly for two years. He was returned as the Liberal member for Banff in the first Alberta general election in November 1905. He sat in the Legislature for fifteen years. In 1906 Fisher was named the Speaker of the Legislature. At the time it as said he was the wealthiest member in the Chamber. He purchased the Speaker's chair himself. In 1907 he married Helen Marjorie Powell, a member of a politically prominent Ottawa family. He died while still a sitting member in 1920.

[See: Canadian Parliamentary Guide, 1920)]

Amedee E. Forget

Born November 12, 1847 at Marieville, Lower Canada, son of Jeremie Forget and Marie Guenette. He was of ethnic French descent and a Roman Catholic. His ancestors came to New France in the late 17th Century. He was related to Senator Louis Joseph Forget (1876-1911). Educated at Marieville College, he then studied law under J.A. Chapleau. He was admitted to the Quebec Bar in 1871. Forget then joined the Dominion civil service. In 1875 he was appointed one of the Commissioners to settle the Metis land claims in the Northwest Territories. Ten years later he was named Commissioner for Indian Affairs. In 1898 Forget was appointed the Lieutenant Governor of the Northwest Territories. He held this position for seven years. Prime Minister Laurier appointed Amedee Emmanuel Forget the first Lieutenant Governor of Alberta in 1910, he settled at Banff. Prime Minister Laurier appointed Forget to the Senate in 1911. He sat in the Red Chamber as an Alberta Senator for twelve years. In 1876 he married Henriette, daughter of Col. C.E. Drolet of Montreal. His wife was an honorary president of the daughters of the Empire and a member of the National Council of Women. Forget died June 8, 1923 at Ottawa at the age of seventy-five.

[See: Who's Who and Why, (1912)]

John Jost Gaetz

Born June 6, 1859, at Grand Banks, Newfoundland, song of Thomas Gaetz and his wife whose maiden was Jost. He was a nephew of Dr. Leo Gaetz, the pioneer Red Deer Methodist Missionary. He was of ethnic German descent and a Methodist. His ancestors came to North American in 1750. He came to Canada as a child of two, attending Mont Allison University. He lived at Seafroth, Ontario, and then at Guysburough, he became a farmer. John Jost Gaetz was returned the Liberal member for Red Deer in the October 28, 1918 by-election. The vacancy occurred when incumbent Edward Michener was summoned to the Senate February 5, 1918. He sat in the Legislature for three years. In 1921 he was defeated by UFA candidate George W. Smith whose wife was a daughter of Dr. Leo Gaetz. He died in 1937 at Red Deer.

[See: Canadian Parliamentary Guide, (1925)]

Robert Gardiner

Born February 24, 1879 in Aberdenshire, Scotland. He was of ethnic Scottish descent and a Presbyterian. He was educated at an elementary rural school. He came to Canada in 1902, homesteading near Excel, Alberta. In time he became a prominent farmer and an active member of the United Famers of Alberta, a grain movement. He was also active in municipal politics, serving as first as councilor and then as a reeve of Golden Centre district from 1914 to 1921. Robert Gardiner was returned the UFA member for the Medicine Hate riding in the June 27, 1921 federal by-election. He was the first member of his protest movement to sit in the House of Commons. He served a total of fifteen years in Parliament and was an active member of the so-called Ginger Group of Progressives that toppled the year old conservative administration of Prim Minister Arthur Meighan in September 1916. In 1932 he was elected the president of the UFA replacing the aged

Henry Wire Wood. In 1935 Gardiner was defeated by Social Creditor Victor Quelch and then retired from politics at the age of fifty-six. He died February 6, 1945 at Calgary.

[See: Canadian Who's Who, (1936)]

Colin Genge

Born in 1860. As a young man he enlisted in the Northwest Mounted Police and served at Fort MacLeod. He was of ethnic Scottish descent and a Presbyterian. 1886 he became a Fort MacLeod hotel proprietor and also was a hardware merchant. In 1900 he served as Mayor of For MacLeod. Colin Genge was returned the Liberal member for MacLeod in 1909. He died in 1910 before he could be sworn in as a member of the Legislature.

Andrew Hill Gilmour

Born in 1875 in Middlesex, Ontario, son of James Gilmour, a farmer, and his wife Sarah Elizabeth McClary. His father was the Conservative member for the Middlesex riding from 1896 to 1904. He was of ethnic Scottish descent and a Presbyterian. He came to Manitoba in 1897. He only stayed briefly before moving to Lacombe, District of Alberta, N.W.T. He became a prominent Lacombe merchant in partnership with William F. Puffer. He was an unsuccessful candidate in 1905. Andrew Gilmour was returned the Conservative member for Lacombe I 1917. He sat in the Legislature as a member of the opposition for four years. In 1921 he was defeated by UFA candidate Mrs. M. Irene Parlby. He died in 1938.

[See: Canadian Parliamentary Guide, (1921)]

John Murray Glendenning

Born May 22, 1872 at Bennington Ontario, son of James Glendenning and his wife Anne Murray. He was of ethnic Scottish descent and a Presbyterian. He came to Northwest Territories with his widowed mother and brothers in 1891. They first ranched near High River. Later John worked first on George Lane's ranch and then Patrick Burns.

In 1904 he established a ranch near Nanton. John M. Glendenning was returned a Liberal member for Nanton in 1909. He sat in the Legislature for eight years as a government backbencher. Hon. Partison Leguer James Weir defeated him in 1917. He was an unsuccessful candidate in 1921. He was living in Nanton in retirement in 1958. He died in 1962.

[See: Canadian Parliamentary Guide, (1917)]

William Antrobus Greisbach, D.S.O., K.C.

Born January 3. 1878 at Fort Qu'Appelle, Northwest Territories, son of Major Jenry Greisbach and his wife Emma Hodgkins. As a young man his father had served in the Prussian army and on coming to Canada in 1874 was the first man to enlist in the newly formed Northwest Mounted Police. He was of German and English descent and an Anglican. Educated at Winnipeg's St. John College, he studied law. At the outbreak of the South African War (Boer War) he enlisted and saw active service with the Canadian Mounted Rifles. After being demobilized he was admitted to the MWT Bar in 1901 and practiced law in Edmonton, becoming the senior partner in the firms of Griesbach, O'Connor and O'Connor. While still in his twenties he served as the mayor of Edmonton. He was an unsuccessful provincial candidate in 1905 and again in 1913. During World War I he served in the Canadian Expeditionary Force on the Western Front where he was awarded the D.S.O. in 1916 and rose to the rank of Brigadier-General. After the war he became the Inspector-General of the Canadian Army for Western Canada, with the rank of Major General. Major Genearl W.A. Griesbach was returned as the Unionist Pro-Government member for the Edmonton West riding in 1917 defeating Liberal incumbent Frank Oliver with the help of the oversea soldiers' vote. He sat in the House of Commons for one term until his appointment to the Senate in 1921. He was an active senator until his death on January 21, 1945 at Ottawa at the age of sixty-seven.

[See: Canadian Who's Who, (1938)]

Peter Gunn

Born February 9, 1864 at Thurso, Carthness, Scotland, song of John Gunn and his wife Barbara. He was of ethnic Scottish descent and a Presbyterian. He was educated at Thurso. He came to Northwest Territories as a young man and worked as a fur trader in the vast region north of Fort Edmonton. In time, he had made his permanent home in Lac St. Anne. He was associated with the Hudson Bay Company for twenty-seven years. He also became a rancher. In 1891 he married a Thurso girl and she travelled with him. One of his daughters married C. Milton McKeen, M.L.A. for Lac St. Anne from 1921 to 1935 and later served as a family court judge at Calgary. Peter Gunn was returned the Liberal member for Lac St. Anne in 1909. He sat in the Legislature for eight years. In 1917 he did not seek re-election but retired from politics at the age of fifty-three. He died in 1927.

[See: Canadian Parliamentary Guide, (1917)]

Howard Hadden Halladay

Born June 15, 1878 at Edgin, Ontario, son of Mack Halladay and his wife Lov Howard. He was of ethnic English descent and a Methodist. He was educated at Athens and Winnipeg. He came to Alberta as a young man, becoming a Hanna insurance agent and farmer. He served as the Mayor of Hanna from 1913 to 1918. Howard H. Halladay was returned the Unionist Pro-Borden government member for the Bow River riding in 1917. He sat in the House of Commons for four years. In 1921 he did not seek re-election but retired from politics at the age of forty-three. Record of death not found.

[See: Canadian Who's Who, (1921)]

William James Harmer

Born October 16, 1872 at Fort Frontenac, near Kingston, Ontario, son of James Harmer and his wife Agatha Walker. He was of ethnic English descent and a Methodist. Educated at Napanee, he trained as a telegraph operator. He came to the Northwest Territories in 1891, settling in Edmonton where he worked in the railway telegraph office. He became the Deputy Minister of Railways under his friends Premier Arthur L. Sifton from 1911 to 1917. On the urging of Premier Sifton, Prime Minister Borden summoned William J. Harmer to the Senate on February 5, 1918. The Calgary Herald declared: "The appointment was an unpleasant surprise... Harmer has performed no public action, nor has he attained any public or personal distinction. The record is that of a civil servant of very ordinary ability, whose chief and only function has been to act as a political manager for Hon. A. L. Sifton." Senate records reveal that Senator Harmer did not speak even once in twenty-nine years in the Red Chamber. He died September 1947 at Napanee, Ontario.

[See: Canadian Who's Who, (1947)]

Horace Harvey, Q.C.

Born in 1863 in Elgin County, Ontario, son of William Harvey and his wife. His father had been a Member of Parliament for East Elgin in the 1870's. He was an Anglican. He attended the University of Toronto, graduating first in Arts and then in Law in 1888. He was admitted to the Ontario Bar in 1889. Coming west, he settled in Calgary and was admitted to the NWT Bar in 1889. He practiced law in Calgary. Harvey joined the federal civil service and was named Registrar of Lands and Titles of Southern Alberta in 1899 and then Deputy Attorney General for the N.W.T. a year later. In 1904 Harvey was appointed a NWT Justice. In 1907 he was transferred to the newly established Alberta Supreme Court as a Justice. In 1910 he became the Chief Justice of the Alberta Supreme Court. This took place in 1924 upon the death of Chief Justice David Scott. Horace Harvey, for the second time, became Chief Justice of Alberta. He was still on the Bench when he died in 1949 at the age of 86. He was the last link with the Northwest Territories administration.

John Herron

Born November 15, 1853 at Ashton, Carleton County, Canada West, son of John Herron and his wife Margaret Ida Lake. He was one of the original North West Mounted Police enlisted in the newly created force. He was a member of the detachment that built Fort MacLeod in 1874, and then built Fort Calgary in 1875. After his discharge from the Force he became a prominent Pincher Creek rancher. He was also a licensed commissioner and federal livestock inspector. During the Northwest Revolt, he raised a militia unit of Rocky Mountain Rangers and saw active service during the campaign. John Herron was returned as the Conservative member for the Alberta riding in 1904. He was re-elected the member for the MacLeod riding in 1908. He sat in the House of Commons as an Opposition member for seven years. While in Parliament, he was the spokesman for the cattle ranchers and their interests. Liberal David E. Warnock defeated him in 1911. He was an unsuccessful federal candidate in 1925 and 1926. He died August 20, 1936 at Pincher Creek.

[See: Who's Who and Why, (1910)]

Cornelius Hiebert

Born August 2, 1862 near the Sea of Azor, Southern Russia, son of John Hiebert and his wife Helena Tows. He was of ethnic Dutch descent and a Mennonite. His ancestors were invited to settle in Russia by the Empress Catherine and the Great in the 18th century. He came to Canada as a child his parents settling Manitoba. As a young man he came with a group of his coreligionists to settle near Didsbury north of Calgary. In time he became a prominent lumber merchant and proprietor of a Knee Hill coal mine. He was the overseer of Village of Didsbury in 1902 and a school Trustee. The Mennonites in the district wanted instruction in school to be German. Cornelius Hebert was returned the Conservative member for Rosebud in the first 1905 Alberta general election. He sat in the Legislature for four years as an opposition member. In 1909 he was an unsuccessful independent candidate for Didsbury, being defeated by Liberal Emmett Stauffer. He then retired from politics.

[See: MacRae. The History of Alberta, (1912)]

James Bismark Holden

Born October 4, 1876 at Singhauton, Ontario, son of James Holden and his wife Sarah Service. His father was a blacksmith. He was of ethnic Scottish descent and a Presbyterian. He was educated at Simcoe County. He came to Manitoba in 1891, working at Vegreville where he became a successful farmer. He also was a real estate agent. From 1915 to 1919 he served as the Mayor of Vegreville. James B. Holden was returned the Liberal member for Vermillion in the July 6, 1906 by-election. He sat in the Legislature for seven years. The last four years as a Vegreville member. In 1913 he did not seek re-election but retired from politics. He was an unsuccessful federal candidate in 1921 and again in 1935. He died April 10, 1955.

[See: Alberta Past and Present, (1924)]

George Edgar Leroy Hudson

Born August 4. 1882 at St. Mary's, Ontario, son of George Hudson and his wife Elizabeth Harrison. He was of ethnic English descent and a Methodist. Educated in Perth County. Came to the Northwest territories as a young man, he homesteaded near Wainwright. He became a well-known farmer. G.E. Leroy Hudson was returned as the Conservative member for Wainwright in 1913. He sat in the Legislature for eight years as a member of the Opposition. At the outbreak of WWI he enlisted in the Canadian Army and went overseas as a Lieutenant with the Canadian Expeditionary Force. He saw active service with the 29th Battalion. In 1921 he was defeated by John Russell Love, the 25 year old U.F.A. candidate and then retired from politics.

[See: Canadian Parliamentary Guide, (1921)]

James Duncan Hyndman

Born July 29, 1874 at Charlottetown, P.E.I., son of Charles Augustus Hyndman and Catherine Macdonald. He was of English and Scottish descent as well an Anglican. Educated at Charlottetown's Prince of Wales College, he read law with A.A. McLean, K.C., who served as the federal member for Queens. He was admitted to the P.E.I. Bar in 1899. In the same year, James Hyndman went to Manitoba where he joined his uncle to form a legal firm in Portage La Prairie. In 1903 he moved to Edmonton becoming the senior partner in the legal firm of Hyndman and Hyndman. He served as a city alderman from 1904 to 1914. Active in federal politics, he was an unsuccessful Conservative candidate for the Sturgeon constituency in 1913. Justice Minister C.J. Doherty appointed James D. Hyndman a Justice of the Alberta Supreme Count: Appellate Division. He retired from the Bench in 1931. In 1902 he had married Ethel Davies, daughter of Sir Louis Davies, a former premier of Prince Edward Island and a Chief Justice of Canada. Two of J.D. Hyndman's grandsons became prominent in provincial politics: L.D. "Lou" Hyndman as an Alberta cabinet minister and Peter Hyndman as a British Columbia cabinet minister. J.D. Hyndman died October 11, 1971 at the age of 97.

[See: Canadian Who's Who, (1967)]

John Henry William Shore Kemmis

Born July 18, 1867 at Oati, Madras, southern India, son of Captain John G. Kemmis and his wife May Needham. He father was an officer in the Indian Army. He was of ethnic English/Anglo-Irish descent and an Anglican. Educated at Dublin, he came to Canada as a young man in 1893 and attended the Ontario Agricultural College at Guelph, Ontario. On the outbreak of the Northwest Rebellion in the spring of 1885, he enlisted with the Moose Mountain Scouts militia unit in Winnipeg and served as a dispatch rider between Calgary and Edmonton through hostile territory. After being demobilized at Regina, he homesteaded in the Fork District near Pincher Creek where he became a prominent rancher. In 1898 he married Maude Elton who had been born at Locknow, India. She was the daughter of a neighboring rancher, Colonel B.W. Elton, a former British army officer. The young couple was married in the same church as his parents, Trinity Church, Bath, Somerset, England. They returned to Canada to establish their home. He was an unsuccessful provincial candidate in 1905. John Henry W.S. Kemmis was returned the Conservative member for the Pincher Creek in the October 1911 by-election. He sat in the Legislature for ten years as the spokesman for cattle ranchers' interests of southern Alberta. In 1921 he did not seek re-election and retired to his ranch. He moved to Calgary in 1925 and died October 13, 1942 at Calgary at the age of 75.

George Lane

Born March 6, 1856 near Des Moines, Iowa son of Joseph Lane and his wife Julia Pidgeon. He was of ethnic English descent and a Methodist. As a young man he became a cowboy. Later he became a ranch foreman in the Montana territory. He came to Canada in 1883; he was hired as the foreman on the Northwest Company ranch. In 1891 he went into the ranching business for himself and fourteen years later purchased the large Bar U Ranch near Pekisko on the Bow river. George Lane was one of the "Big Four" ranchers with Pat Burns, A.J. McLean, and A. Ernest Cross that bank rolled the first Calgary Stampede. George Lane was returned as the Liberal member of Bow Valley in 1913. However, he vacated his seat to permit C.R. Mitchell to re-enter the Chamber. He died April 24, 1925 near Pekisko at the age of fifty-nine.

[See: MacRae. The History of Alberta, (1912)]

Frank S. Leffinwell

Born November 16, 1868 at Wjotewater, Wosconsin, son of Seth Leffingwell and his wife Helen Weston. He was an American of ethnic English descent whose ancestors immigrated to New England in the 1660's. He came to Canada in 1896, when he settled at Warner near the Canadian-American border and was employed to help new homesteaders. He was the proprietor of the Warner Hotel. He also was a real estate agent and a farmer. Frank S. Leffinwell was returned as the Liberal member for Warner in 1913. He sat in the Legislature for eight years as a government backbencher. He was the spokesman for recently arrived Americans. In 1921 he was defeated by U.F.A. American-born Maurice J. Connor and then retired from politics at the age of fifty-three. He died in 1945.

[See: Canadian Parliamentary Guide, (1921)]

Senator James Alexander Lougheed

Born September 1, 1854 at Brampton, Upper Canada, son of John Lougheed and his wife Mary. Educated at Toronto and called to the Bar of Ontario in 1877. In 1883 he settled at Calgary where he was called to the Bar of the Northwest Territories. In 1884 he married Isabella "Bell" Hardisty, daughter of William Hardisty, Chief Factor of the Hudson's Bay Company and grand-daughter of Richard Hardisty, also a facto of the Hudson's Bay Company. Prime Minister John A. Macdonald named James Alexander Lougheed Alberta's second senator in 1889. He sat in the upper chamber for 37 years. In 1906 he became the Conservative leader of the Senate Opposition. Five hears later when Robert Borden became Prime Minister, Lougheed was named to the cabinet as Minister Without Portfolio and government leader in the Senate. In 1920 Prime Minister Arthur Meighen appointed Senator Lougheed to office in December 1921. He died on November 3, 1925 at Ottawa at the age of 71. His funeral was held at Calgary's Holy Redeemers Cathedral and one of the largest in the city's history. His grandson is E. Peter Lougheed.

[See: Who's Who and Why, (1912)]

James Robert Lowery, B.A.

Born April 12, 1884 at Wellmans Corners, Ontario, son of John B. Lowery and his wife Rachel. He was of ethnic Ulster Scott descent and a Presbyterian. Educated at Frankford, he attended Queen's University. Upon arriving in Alberta he became a Lloydminster merchant. He was an unsuccessful candidate in 1909. He attended the University of Alberta graduating in Arts in 1914. James R. Lowery was returned as the Conservative member for Alexandra in 1913. He sat in the Legislature for eight years as an Opposition member. At the outbreak of WWI, he enlisted in the Canadian Army. He went overseas as a major with the 49th Battalion and saw active service at Kimy Ridge in 1916. In 1921 he did not seek re-election but retired from politics. In 1957 he was living on the coast.

[See: Canadian Parliamentary Guide, (1921)]

Frederick W. Lundy

Born November 10, 1878 on a farm in Peel County, near Brampton, Ontario, son of Joseph Lundy and his wife Elizabeth Arthur. He was of ethnic English descent and a Methodist. Educated at Brampton, he attended Toronto's Osgoode Hall Law School, graduating in 1905. He was admitted to the Ontario Bar. He came to Alberta in 1908, he settled at Stony Plain where he became a prominent lawyer. Frederick W. Lundy acted for four years as an opposition member. In 1921 he was defeated in his re-election bid by U.F.A. candidate Wilbert M. Washburn and retired from politics.

[See: Blue. Alberta: Past Present, (1924)]

Roberta Catherine MacAdam

Born June 21, 1881 at Sarnia, Ontario, daughter of Robert MacAdam, a newspaper publisher, and his wife Catherine Brown. She was an Anglican of Anglo-Irish descent on her paternal side. Educated at Guelph, she attended Chicago University. As a young woman, she came to Alberta and settled at Edmonton where she was in charge of "the domestic science" department of the government. She also helped in the establishment of Women's Institutes across rural Alberta. At the outbreak of World War I, Miss MacAdam enlisted in the cursing corps. She received a commission and went overseas with the Canadian Expeditionary Force. Lt. MacAdam served in the United Kingdom. In the Special Overseas Solider legislative election to send two service personnel to the Legislature, Lt. MacAdam and Padre Captian (Methodist) Robert Pearson were returned. Initially she sat as Miss MacAdam, but on September 21, 1920 she married her brother's law partner, Harvey Simpson Stinson Price, of Calgary. In 1921 she did not seek re-election and retired from provincial politics. The Prices homesteaded for a decade in the Peace River Country before finally settling in Calgary.

[See: Canadian Parliamentary Guide, (1921)]

Archibald John McArthur

Born February 21, 1857 on the Isle of Iona, Hebrides Scotland, son of Peter McArthur and his wife Mary Macdonald. He was of ethnic Scottish descent and a Baptist. He came to Canada as a child, raised in Ontario's Bruce County. He was educated at Paisley. He became a lumber merchant and livestock exporter from Ontario to the Canadian Prairies. He came to the Northwest Territories in 1887, he settled at Calgary where he became a prominent citizen. Archibald J. McArthur was returned as a Liberal member in the October 3 1910 Gleinein by-election. He died while still an incumbent June 5th 1911.

Maitland Stewart McCarthy

Born February 15, 1872 at Orangeville, Ontario, song of Judge Bolton McCarthy and his wife Frances Stewart. He was of Anglo-Irish descent and an Anglican. Educated at Port Hope, he attended the University of Toronto, graduating in arts and then law. He was admitted to the Ontario Bar in 1897 and practiced law in Laughton County. In 1900 he married Eva Florence Watson of Hamilton. They moved to Alberta in 1903 and settled in Calgary where he practiced law. M.S. McCarthy was returned as the Conservative member for Calgary riding in 1904 and sat in the House of Commons as an opposition member for seven years. In 1911 he did not seek re-election. Justice Minister C.J. Doherty appointed M.S. McCarthy as a Justice of Alberta Supreme Court in 1914. When the courts were reorganized in 1921 he was transferred to the Alberta Supreme Court: Trial Division. He retired from the Bench in 1926 and died May 17, 1930 at Montreal at the age of fifty-eight.

[See: Canadian Who's Who, (1912)]

Matthew McCauley

Born July 11, 1850 at Owen Sound, Canada West son of Alexander McCauley and his wife Eleanor. Educated at Owen Sound, he then farmed in Grey County. He came to Manitoba in 1871, where he worked as a laborer in Winnipeg. Later he was the proprietor of a garbage firm. He came to the Northwest Territories in 1870, settling at Fort Edmonton where he was a trader where homesteading near For Saskatchewan. Later he became a building contractor and owner of Cartage Company. McCauley was the first mayor of Edmonton in 1892. During the Northwest Revolt of 1885, he organized a "homeguard" in the settlement. Matthew McCauley was the member for Edmonton in the N.W.T. Assembly from 1895 to 1902 and he was returned the Liberal member for Vermillion in the first Alberta General Election in November 1905. He vacated his seat the next year on his appointment as the Warden of the Edmonton Penitentiary. He held this position for six years before retiring in 1912. McCauley, even though he was in his sixties, then became a Peace River pioneer, homesteading at Sexsmith. He died October 25, 1920 at Sexsmith, Alberta at the age of seventy.

[See: Canadian Parliamentary Guild, (1905)]

John Arthur McColl

Born February, 21, 1875 at Maxville, Glengarry County, Ontario, son of Neil McCall and his wife Anne McDougall. He was of ethnic Scottish descent and a Congregationalist. He was educated at Maxville. He came to the Northwest Territories as a young man, he homesteaded in Collholme in eastern Alberta. In time he became a prominent farmer. John A. McColl was returned the Liberal member for Acadia in 1913. He sat in the Legislature for eight years as a government backbencher. In 1921 he did not seek re-election but retired from politics at the age of forty-six.

[See: Canadian Parliamentary Guide, (1921)]

Gordon Macdonald

He was of ethnic Scottish descent and a Presbyterian. He became a Belvedere farmer. Gordon MacDonald was returned as the Liberal member for Pembina in 1913. He sat in the Legislature for eight years as a government backbencher. At the outbreak of World War I he enlisted in the Canadian Army. He went overseas with the Canadian Expeditionary Force as a Lieutenant with the 49th Battalion. He saw active service on the Western Front during the Vimy Ridge campaign in 1917. In 1921 he did not seek re-election but retired from politics.

[See: Canadian Parliamentary Guide, (1921)]

John Alexander McDougall

Born May 20, 1854 at Oakwood, Canada West, son of Alex McDougall and his wife Janet Cumming. He was of ethnic Scottish descent and a Presbyterian. By 1870 he was a store clerk at Woodville. He came to Manitoba in 1873 and was employed to copy land surveyors' field notes in the Winnipeg's Lands Title office and in the winter attended Manitoba College at Kildonan. Later he became a trader. He became the Edmonton director of the Northern Crown Bank. He was mayor of Edmonton in 1897 and again in 1908. John A MacDougall was returned the Liberal member for Edmonton 1909. He sat in the Legislature for four years as a government backbencher. He died in 1928 at Edmonton.

[See: MacRae. The History of Alberta, (1912)]

Wilbert McIntyre

Born July 15. 1867 at Rosedale, Ontario, son of John McIntyre and his wife Anne Umphries. He was born into a wealthy family. He was of ethnic Scottish descent and a Presbyterian. Educated at Owen Sound, he attended the University of Toronto, graduating in Medicine. He became a physician. He came to the Northwest Territories as a young man, where he settled at Strathcona, South Edmonton where he became a prominent physician and surgeon. Dr. Wilbert McIntyre was returned as the Liberal member for the Strathcona riding in April 5, 1905 by-election. The previous member, Peter Talbot, was summoned to the Senate, and caused the vacancy. He sat in the House of Commons until the time of his death. He died July 21, 1909 at Strathcona at the age of forty-two. He was named the president of the Northern Alberta Medical Association in 1906.

[See: Canadian Parliamentary Guide, (1909)]

Alexander Grant MacKay, M.A., K.C.

Born March 7 1860 at Sydenham, Ontario, son of Hugh MacKay and his wife Catherine McInnis. He was of ethnic Scottish descent and a Presbyterian. Educated at Owen Sound, he attended the University of Toronto, graduating with a masters of Arts degree. He became a North Grey layer. Alexander G. MacKay was returned as the Liberal member for North Grey in 1902. He sat in the Ontario Legislature for nine years. He served as the leader of the Opposition for three years. MacKay vacated his seat and moved to Edmonton in 1911. Alexander G. MacKay was returned the Liberal member for Athabasca in 1913. He sat in the Legislature for seen years. In 1918 Premier Stewart appointed him to the Cabinet as the Minister of Municipal Affairs and later Minister of Health. He died in 1920 while will a sitting member at the age of sixty.

[See: Who's Who and Why, (1912)]

Arthur Henry Mackie

Born in 1844, son of Joseph Ignatius Mackie, a notary public and deputy registrar of Cookshire, Quebec, and his wife Clothilde Lantague of Stukely, Quebec. He was of ethnic Irish-French descent and a Roman Catholic. Arthur H Mackie became a prominent Edmonton lawyer. For many years he was the senior partner in the legal firm of Mackie and Cormack. In 1917 he was nominated the Unionist candidate for the newly formed Edmonton East federal riding. His opponent was A.E. May who supported Laurier and his anti-conscription stand. Mackie was returned by a large majority. Of the Edmonton East soldiers serving in the Canadian Expeditionary Force in the United Kingdom and on the Western Front, 1900 voted for Mackie and 100 voted for May. Arthur H. Mackie was the first Roman Catholic member of the House of Commons from Alberta. He sat in Parliament for four years. In 1921 he did not seek re-election but retired fro m politics. For years his legal partner was John Cormack.

[See: Canadian Parliamentary Guide, (1921)]

Joseph Seeley McCallum

Born July 9, 1884 at Renfrew, Ontario, son of Angus McCallum and is wife Jane Seeley. He was of ethnic Scottish descent and a Protestant. He came to the Northwest Territories as a child, he was educated at Beaver Lake and Edmonton. He taught as a young man in rural school. He became a livestock dealer and agricultural machinery dealer at Mundare. In 1905 he married Catherine, daughter of Malcolm McCallum. Joseph S. McCallum was returned the Liberal member for Vegreville in 1913. He was the youngest member in the Chamber. He sat in the Legislature for eight years as a private member. In 1921 he was defeated by U.F.A. candidate Archibald M. Matheson, and then retired from politics.

Henry W. McKenny

Born February 24, 1848 at Amherstburg, Upper Canada, song of Augustus McKenny and his wife Mathilda Grandin. His mother was of Norman ancestry who ancestors came to New France in the late 17th century. He was of ethnic Irish descent and a Roman Catholic. He came to Manitoba as a child and was educated at Winnipeg. He became a trader in the Northwest Territories, finally settling at Fort Edmonton where he became a trader in the Northwest Territories, finally settling at Fort Edmonton where he had visited in 1875. Later he became a prominent St. Albert merchant and postmaster. He retired from business in 1903 Henry W. McKenny was returned the Liberal member for St. Alberta in 1905, for Pembina and 1909, and again for Clearwater in 1913. He sat for twelve years in the Legislature as one of the most colorful members. In 1917 he did not seek re-election but retired from politics at the age of sixty-nine. He died in 1925 at St. Albert. Often H.W. McKenny was referred to as a French Canadian politician rather than an English one.

[See: <u>Canadian Parliamentary Guide</u>, (1917)

Malcolm McKenzie

Born May 31, 1953 at Kincardine, Canada West. He was of ethnic Scottish descent and a Presbyterian. Educated at Bruce County, he attended Queen's University graduated in Law. He came to the Northwest territories in 1888, he settled at Fort MacLeod where he became the junior partner in the legal firm of Haultain and McKenzie. Malcolm McKenzie was returned as the Liberal member for MacLeod in 1905. He sat in the Legislature for eight years. From 1912 to 1913, he served as the Provincial Treasurer in Premier Sifton's cabinet. He died March 15, 1913 while still a sitting member at the age of forty-nine.

Louise McKinney (nee Crummy)

Born September 22, 1868 at Frankville, Ontario, daughter of Richard Crummy and his wife Esther Empey. She was of ethnic Anglo-Irish descent and a Methodist. Educated at Athens, she attended the Ottawa Normal School, qualifying as a teacher. She taught school before her marriage to James McKinney in 1896. The McKinneys came to the Northwest Territories, settling at Claresholm. McKinney became a successful farmer. Mrs. McKinney became active in the Prohibition movement and prominent in the Women's Christian Temperance Union. Louise McKinney was returned the "Non-Partisan" member for Claresholm in 1917. She was the first woman ever to be nominated to a Canadian Legislature. She defeated William Moffat. At the time, it was said that there was only one gentleman in Alberta- William Moffat because he had given up his seat in the Legislature to a "lady". In 1921 she was defeated in the re-election bid by Independent farmer Thomas C. Milner and returned from politics. Later she was the only woman to sign the papers that created the United Church of Canada in 1925 and was one of the seven Alberta Women that won their case in front of the British Privy Council that women were persons and so could be summoned to sit in the Senate in London in 1929.

[See: Canadian Parliamentary Guide, (1921)]

Archibald J. McLean

Born September 26, 1860 in Elgin County, Canada West, son of James McLean and his wife Murchie. His parents had been born in Scotland. He was of ethnic Scottish descent and a Presbyterian. He was also a Freemason. As a young man he moved to Manitoba where became a large raiser of livestock. In 1897 McLean purchased a large Taber ranch and became one of the wealthiest Southern Alberta ranchers. In 1912, he with Pat Burns, A. Ernest Cross and George Lane financed the first Calgary Stampede. He was also a coalmine proprietor. Archibald J. McLean was returned as the Independent Liberal candidate for Lethbridge district in 1909. He was re-elected as the Liberal member for Taber in 1913. He sat in the Legislature for twelve years. Premier Sifton appointed him to the Cabinet in 1910 as the Provincial Secretary. A year later he was transferred to the Municipal Affairs portfolio. In 1921 he was defeated in the re-election bid by U.F.A. candidate Lawrence Peterson, and retired to his ranch. He died in 1933.

[See: Canadian Parliamentary Guide, (1921)]

Dr. John Robert McLeod

Born January 20, 2973 at Zorra, Ontario, son of William C. McLeod and his wife Mary Catherine McKay. He was of ethnic Scottish descent and a Presbyterian. Educated at Woodstock, he qualified as a teacher. He taught in rural Oxford County for several years. He then attended the Detroit Medical College, graduating as a physician in 1896. He then served as a medical health officer in Michigan for three years. He came to the Northwest Territories in 1901, settling at Edberg where he practiced his profession. Dr. John R. McLeod was returned the Liberal member for Ponoka in 1905. He sat in the Legislature for four years as a government backbencher. In 1909 he did not seek re-election from politics and retired at the age of thirty-seven. He died 1931.

[See: Canadian Parliamentary Guide, (1909)]

Donald McNabb

Born in 1870 in Scotland, his father was a coal miner. He was of ethnic Scottish descent and a Presbyterian. At the age of fourteen he started to work in the coalmines at the side of his father. Coming to the Northwest Territories in 1903, he settled at Lethbridge where he worked as a coalminer and became a union official. Active in civic politics, he served as a Labor alderman on the city counsel. He also held a homestead near Taber. In January 1909 he returned as the Labor member for Lethbridge by acclamation. He sat for one session of the Legislature as an Opposition member. In the April 1909 general election, he was defeated by Liberal W.A. Buchanan, the Lethbridge Herald Publishers, and retired from politics at the age of thirty-nine. He died in 1934 at Lethbridge at the age of sixty-four.

[See: Lethbridge Herald, (January 1909)]

James McNaughton

Born March 10, 1864 in Glengarry County, Canada West, son of Alexander McNaughton and his wife Catherine Kennedy. He was of ethnic Scottish descent and a Presbyterian. He became a wealthy Ontario merchant. Upon retiring, he came to the Northwest Territories where he settled at Carmongon, a district of Alberta. James McNaughton was returned the Liberal member for Little Bow in 1913. He sat in the Legislature eight years as a government backbencher. In 1921 he was defeated in his re-election bid by U.F.A. candidate O.L. "Tory" McPherson and then retired from politics at the age of fifty-seven. He died in 1959 at the advanced age of ninety-five. He is the only member to refer to himself as a 'gentleman'.

[See: Canadian Parliamentary Guide, (1921)]

John Allan McPherson

Born December 28, 1855 at Mont Pleasant, Canada West, son of Donald McPherson and his wife Catherine McPherson. He was of ethnic Scottish descent and a Presbyterian. He came to Manitoba in 1878, he was employed as a railway construction worker. In 1881, he made the 1,000 mile trek to Fort Edmonton with an ox cart. The trip took 105 days. Young McPherson homesteaded near Spruce Grove's first post master in 1897. John A. McPherson was returned the Liberal member for Stony Plain in 1905. He sat in the Legislature for eight years as a government backbencher. In 1913 he was defeated by Conservative Conrad Wieder Hammer and then retired from politics at the age of fifty-seven. He died December 29, 1924 at Spruce Grove.

[See: Canadian Parliamentary Guide, (1912)]

Charles Alexander Magrath

Born April 22, 1860 at North Augusta, Upper Canada, son of Bolton Magrath and his wife Laura McPhee. He was of Anglo-Irish descent and an Anglican. He came to the Northwest Territories in 1878 where he became a Dominion topographical surveyor. In 1885 he settled in Lethbridge where he acted as an irrigation engineer. Active in civic politics, her served as the first mayor of Lethbridge. Magrath married twice: his first wife was Margaret Muir, daughter of Alexander Muir, composer of "The Maple Leaf Forever"; his second wife was Mabel Gault, daughter of Sir William Gault, one of the Fathers of Confederation. C.A. Magrath was returned to the N.W.T. Legislative Assembly as the member for Lethbridge in 1891. He sat in the Assembly for seven years. In the 1908 federal election he was returned as the member for the Medicine Hat riding and sat in the House of Commons for three years. In 1911 he was defeated by Liberal publisher W.A. Buchanan and retired from politics at the age of 51. From 1914 to 1935 he served as the chairman of the Canadian-United States International Boundary Commission. In 1927 he was elected fellow of the Royal Society of Canada. He was the author of <u>Canadian Growth and Some Problems Affecting It</u> (Ottawa, 1910) and <u>The Gaults, Father and Son, Pioneers in the Development of Southern Alberta</u> (Lethbridge, 1935). He died October 20 1949 at Victoria, British Columbia.

[See: <u>Canadian Who's Who</u>, (1948); <u>MacMillan Dictionary of Canadian</u>, (1978)]

John Plummer Marcellus

Born July 26, 1840 at Williamburg, Upper Canada, son of George W. Marcellus and his wife Luney Low. He was of ethnic Scottish descent and a Presbyterian. His ancestors were of United Empire Loyalist stock, originating from New York state. He worked at a Williamburg farm for years. Arriving in the Northwest Territories in 1888, he became a Pincher Creek horse rancher. He supplied the Northwest Mounted Police with remounts. He grew the Chicago World's Fair of 1893 prize winning heat seeds. John P. Marcellus was returned the Liberal member for Pincher Creek in 1905. He sat in the Legislature for four years as a government backbencher. In 1909 he did not seek re-election but retired at the age of sixty-eight. He died May 29, 1932 at the advanced age of ninety-one.

[See: Canadian Parliamentary Guide, (1909)]

Duncan McLean Marshall

Born September 24, 1872 in Bruce County, Ontario, son of John Marshall and his wife Margaret McMuchy. His father was a farmer. He was of ethnic Scottish descent and a Presbyterian. He was educated at Owen Sound. From 1891 to 1898, he was a prominent organizer in the Patron of the Industry movement across Ontario. He became the publisher of newspapers in Thornbury, Clarksburg and Bracebridge. He was an unsuccessful federal candidate in 1904. Arriving in the Northwest Territories in June 1905, he settled at Edmonton where he became managing editor of the Edmonton Bulletin. He also became a proprietor of a large Olds farm and the publisher of the Olds Gazette. Duncan M. Marshall was returned as Liberal meme for Olds in 1909. He sat in the Legislature for twelve years. Premier Rutherford appointed him the Minister of Agriculture on November 1, 1909. He held this portfolio under Premier Sifton and Premier Stewart. In 1921 he was defeated by U.F.A. candidate Nelson S. Smith. Later he returned to Ontario. Duncan M. Marshall was returned to the Ontario Agriculture. Prime Minister McKenzie King summoned him to the Senate in 1938.

[See: Canadian Who's Who, (1938)]

George S. Mills

Born January 17, 1876 at Oxford, Ontario, son of Albert E. Mills and his wife Sarah Harper. He was of ethnic Irish descent and a Presbyterian. He was also a Freemason. He was educated at Brigden. He became a Lumbton County farmer. He served on the county where he became a prominent farmer. He served a term as the Mayor of Athabasca. George Mills was returned as the Liberal meme for Athabasca in the 1920 by-election. The by-election had been caused by the death of A.G. MacKay, the Minister of health. Mills sat in the Legislature for six years. In the 1926 election, Mills, running as an Independent Liberal was defeated by the "official" Liberal candidate John W. Frame and then retired from politics at the age of fifty-two.

[See: Canadian Parliamentary Guide, (1926)]

Charles R. Mitchell, K.C.

Born November 30, 1872 at Newcastle, New Brunswick, son of James Mitchell and his wife Isabella McCurdy. His father served as the sheriff of Northumberland County. He was of ethnic Scottish descent. He was the nephew of Senator Peter M. Mitchell (1824-1898) one of the Fathers of Confederation and an industrialist. Charles Mitchell attended the University of New Brunswick and the University of King's College, qualifying as a lawyer. He was admitted to the new Brunswick Bar in 1897. He came to the Northwest Territories, becoming a Medicine Hat lawyer. He was appointed a Calgary District Court Judge in 1907. He vacated his seat on the Bench in 1910. Charles was returned as the Liberal member for Medicine Hat and became Premier Sifton's Attorney General and Minister of Education. In 1913 he was defeated in his re-election bid but re-entered the Legislature in the Boy Valley Legislature for sixty years. Until 1921 he was a cabinet minister. In 1925 he was the head of the Opposition. Mitchell vacated his seat on his appointment as a Justice of the Alberta Supreme Court: Appellate Division in March 1926. Ten years later he was transferred to the Trial Division as the Chief Justice. Chief Justice Charles R. Mitchell died August 16, 1942 after a long illness.

[See: Canadian Who's Who, (1938)]

Edward Michener

Born August 18, 1869 at Tintern, Ontario, son of Jacob Michener and his wife Elizabeth Patterson. He was of English descent and a strong Methodist. Educated at St. Catherine, he attended Victoria University graduating in Arts, and Wesley College, Winnipeg, graduating in Divinity. In 1897 he married Mary E. Roland. They had four sons and four daughters. One son, D. Roland Michener, served as the Governor General of Canada from 1967 to 1974. One of his daughters married Errick French Willn, Lieutenant Governor of Manitoba from 1960 to 1965. He worked in the Red Deer Methodist Mission for seven years.

Later he became an investment dealer. He served as the Red Deer mayor for three terms. Edward M. Michener was returned the Independent Conservative Member for Red Deer in 1909. Two years later he became the Leader of the Opposition in the Legislature. He sat in the Chamber until he was summoned to the Senate on February 5, 1918. Senator Michener died June 16, 1947 at Ottawa.

[See: Canada's Who's Who, (1936)]

Wiliam Moffatt

Born January 20, 1849 at Carlton Place, Ottawa, son of Robert Moffat and his Irish wife Mary Ann Saunders. He was of Scottish descent and a Presbyterian. Educated at Carlton Place. He came to Manitoba in 1887, farming near Pilot Mound. He arrived in the Northwest Territories in 1901, he was the first settler at what became Claresholm, half way along the Fort MacLeod, Calgary Trail. It became the jumping off point for homesteaders moving eastward into the Vulcan sea. Moffat became a lumber merchant and also a general merchant. He became a wealthy man. He was the community's first overseer and later the mayor. William Moffat at the age of sixty was returned the Liberal member for the newly established Claresholm Constituency in 1913. He sat in the Legislature for three years as a representative of the lately arrived Southern Alberta homesteaders and the powerful lumber merchants' interest. In 1917 he was defeated by Louise McKinney, the non-Partison League candidate and then retired from politics. R.C. Body Edward said in The Eye Opener at the time Mr. Moffatt was the only gentleman in the Legislature; He gave up his seat to a lady. He died in 1925 at Claresholm.

[See: MacRae. History of Alberta, (1912)]

Hugh John Montgomery

Born July 31, 1876 at Badeque, P.E.I., son of James Montgomery and his wife Kate McFarlane. He was of ethnic Scottish descent and a Presbyterian. He attended Charlottetown Business College. He came to the Northwest Territories as a young man, settling at Wetaskiwin in 1911 and then from 1922 to 1929. Hugh J. Montgomery was returned as the Liberal member for Wetaskiwin in 1913. He sat a total of thirteen years in the candidate for the Alberta Liberal leadership in 1929. In 1935 he was defeated in his re-election bid by Social Creditor John A. Wingblade and then retired from politics at the age of fifty-nine. He died in 1956.

[See: Canadian Parliamentary Guide, (1935), Blue, Alberta: Past and Present (1924)]

Alexander Moore

Born October 1, 1874 at Lion's Head, Ontario, son of Robert Moore and his wife Isabella Kidd. He was of ethnic Welsh-Scottish descent and a Presbyterian. He was also a Freemason. His ancestors had been pioneer settlers on Bruce Peninsula. He came to the Northwest Territories as a young man and settled near Cochrane where he became a prominent farmer. He was active in the United Farmers of Alberta rain movement and served as director. Alexander Moore was returned the U.F.A. member for Cochrane in the November 3. 1920 by-election. The vacancy had been caused by the death of C.W. Fisher, long-time Speaker of the Legislature. He sat in the Legislature for six years in 1926. Due to rain and the muddy condition of the roads, Moore failed to hand his nomination papers to the Returning Officer. At the last moment Moore's campaign manager Robert M. McCool filed nomination papers in his own name. McCool went on to win the seat while Moore, rather unhappily retired from politics. He died 1952.

[See: Canadian Parliamentary Guide, (1926)]

John T. Moore

Born July 3. 1844 in York County, Upper Canada, son of William K. Moore and his wife Isabella. He was of ethnic Irish descent and a Methodist. Educated at Berlin (Kitchener) and Toronto, he became a chartered accountant. He was a very wealthy businessman and land promoter. He came to the Northwest Territories in 1879, where he settled at Red Deer. He became a farmer and livestock breeder who encouraged many Ontarians to settle in the Red Deer district. He was the president of the railway construction that built the Calgary to the

Strathcona Edmonton railway in the early 1890's. John T. Moore was returned the Liberal member for Red Deer in 1905 by defeating Conservative Dr. Leo Gaetz. He sat in the Legislature for four years as a private member on the government side of the Chamber. He was a brilliant public speaker and was referred to as "Silver Tongue Moor". He was defeated in his re-election bid in 1909 by Independent Edward Michener and retired to Toronto. John T. Moore died on June 5, 1917 at Toronto.

[See: Who's Who and Why, (1912)]

Daniel Joakim Morberg

Born August 2, 1870 at Kjose, Denmark, son of Carl W. Morkberg and his wife who maiden name was Seidenfaden. He was of ethnic Scandinavian descent and a Lutheran. He was also a Freemason. He came to Canada as a young man and in 1898 he homesteaded near Markes, District of Alberta, N.W.T. In time he became a prominent dairy farmer. Daniel J. Morkberg was returned as the Liberal member for Innisfail in 1917. He sat in the Legislature for four years as a government backbencher. In 1921 he was defeated in his re-election bid by U.F.A. Donald Cameron and then retired from politics at the age of fifty-one. He was an unsuccessful candidate in 1926 and again in 1930. He died in 1963.

[See: Canadian Parliamentary Guide, (1921)]

Charles McNamara O'Brien

Born March 2, 1875 at Bell Rapids, Ontario, son of J.P. O'Brien and his wife Matilda. He was of ethnic Irish descent and a life-long socialist. He had little formal education. As a young man he worked as a labourer on the railway construction gangs, lumber camps and as a coalminer across Canada. He was a prominent union organizer and an authority on Marxist economic theories. Upon arriving in Alberta, he worked as a miner and union organizer in the Crowsnest coalfield where 80 percent of the miners were unionized. Charles M. O'Brien was returned the Social (Communist) member for Rocky Mountain 1909. He sat in the Legislature for four years as one of the most vocal members of the Opposition. He still holds the unofficial record for delivering the longest speech in the history of the Legislature. In 1913 he was defeat by Robert E. Campbell. Later he moved to the United States where he was a founding member of the American Communist Party.

Charles Herman Olin

Born August 31, 1867 at Westergothland, Sweden, son of Olaf Olin and his wife Sharlotte. He was of ethnic Scandinavian descent and a Lutheran. He came to the United States as a child and was educated in Nebraska. He came to Canada from there in 1892, becoming a Wetaskiwin early pioneer building contractor and farmer. He served as a bridge inspector from 1898 to 1908. Charles H. Olin was returned the Liberal member for Wetaskiwin in 1909. He sat in the Legislature as a government backbencher for five years. He died in 1914 at Wetaskiwin while still a sitting member at the age of fifty-four.

[See: MacRae. The History of Alberta, (1912)]

Alphaeus Patterson

Born March 15, 1855 at Kemptville, Upper Canada son of John Patterson and Martha Tackabery. He was a Methodist. He was named after an early Roman martyr St. Alphauus. Educated at Kemptville, he became a farmer. In the 1890's he was connected with shipping of livestock from Ontario to newly established Alberta homesteaders. He came to the Northwest Territories in 1901 and was the proprietor of an Edmonton concrete company for a decade. One of the early Peace River pioneers, he was the first postmaster of Peace River town in 1911. He owned a farm and published a newspaper. Alphaeus Patterson was returned the Conservative member for Peace River in deferred September 2, 1913 election. He sat in the Legislature for four years as a private member on the Opposition benches. In 1917 he did not seek re-election but retired from politics at the age of sixty-two.

Robert Patterson

Born April 11, 1855 in County Tipperary, Ireland, son of George Patterson and his wife Mary. He was an Anglican of Anglo-Irish descent and an Anglican. He was a cousin of Judge Wright. Educated at Kilkenny, at the age of twenty-one he came to Canada and enlisted in the Northwest Mounted Police. He served at Fort MacLeod. In 1880 he left the force and became a cattle and horse rancher near Fort MacLeod. He built the first brick residence in the community. Robert Patterson was returned as the Conservative member for MacLeod in the October 1910 by-election. He sat in the Legislature as an opposition member for seven years. In 1917, he was defeated in his re-election bid by George Skelding, a coal merchant. He then retired from politics at the age of 61. He died in 1938.

[See: Who's Who and Why, (1913)]

Captain Robert Pearson

Born May 18, 1879 at Ethel, Ontario, son of Robert Pearson and his wife Susan Murgrove. He was of ethnic English descent and a Methodist. He also was a Freemason. Educated at Listowel, he attended the University of Toronto, graduating with an Arts degree. He became a Methodist Minister and was associated with the Y.M.C.A. movement. He had a special interest in athletic activities. At the outbreak of World War I, he enlisted in the Canadian Army as a Methodist padre with the rank of Captain. He served in the Canadian Expeditionary Force overseas on the Western Front with the 49th Battalion. In the special summer 1917 Overseas Soldiers (Province-at-wide) election to elect two representatives, Captain Pearson was returned as an Independent. The other was Lt. Roberta C. McAdams. Captain Pearson sat in the Legislature for nine years. In 1921 he had been re-elected as an Independent Calgary member. In 1926 he did not seek re-election but was appointed Alberta film censor (his cousin was Walt Disney). He held this post for nine years. He died in 1956.

[See: Canadian Parliamentary Guide, (1926)]

Charles S. Pingle

Born October 16, 1880 at Morris, Manitoba, son of Warren Hume Pingle and his wife Georgina. He was of ethnic English descent and an Anglican. He was also a Freemason. Educated at Winnipeg, he became a pharmacist. As a young man he moved to Medicine Hat where he became a prominent businessman. He served as a city alderman from 1910 to 1912. Charles S. Pingle was returned as the Liberal member for Redcliff in 1913. He sat in the Legislature for eight years. From 1919 to 1921 he was the Speaker of the Legislature. In 1921 he was defeated but was once more returned as a member for Medicine Hat in the 1925 by-election. The vacancy had been caused by the death of incumbent William G. Johnson. During World War I he enlisted in the Canadian Army and was part of the Canadian Expeditionary Force while serving as a captain with the 3rd Canadian Mounted Rifles. He saw active service on the Western Front in 1915 to 1916. He was seriously wounded. Captain Pingle died while still a sitting member in the Legislature in 1928. On the death of C.W. Fisher, Captain Charles S. Pingle was named the second Speaker of the Alberta Legislature in 1920.

[See: Canadian Parliamentary Guide, (1921)]

Edward Hulburd Prudden

Born September 28, 1859 at Lockport, New York State, son of Henry Prudden and his wife Saraph Hulbard. On both sides, his ancestors were New England Puritans who arrived in New Haven in 1637. He was of ethnic English descent and a Methodist. He was a Freemason and was educated at Medina, N.Y. As a young man in 1885 he settled in Nebraska where he farmed for seventeen years. He came to Canada in 1902, he homesteaded at Botha, south east of Edmonton. He became a successful farmer. Edward H. Prudden was returned as the Liberal member for Stettler in 1917. He sat in the Legislature for four years as a government backbencher. In 1921 he was defeated by U.F.A. candidate Albert L. Sanders and then retired from politics at the age of sixty-two. He died in 1932.

[See: Canadian Parliamentary Guide, (1921)]

William Franklin Puffer

Born November 1, 1861 at Westport, Canada West, son of Asa Puffer and his wife Louise Cardelia Root. He was of ethnic Scottish descent and a Methodist. His ancestors were United Empire Loyalist Stock. The Puffer family moved to the United States in 1975 where his father farmed in Michigan. He came to the Northwest Territories in 1889, first farming near Calgary. Later he homesteaded near Olds. He in partnership with Andrew Gilmour became prominent Lumber merchants. He was also a cattle dealer and a butcher. William F. Puffer was returned the Liberal member for Olds in 1905. He sat in the Legislature for eight years as a government backbencher. His partner Conservative Andrew H. Gilmour defeated him in 1913. He was an unsuccessful federal candidate in 1917. He died April 22, 1948 at Olds.

[See: Canadian Parliamentary Guide, (1913)]

James Ramsey

Born April 4, 1864 at Imlay City, Michigan son of John Ramsey and his wife Agnes Davidson. He was an American of ethnic Scottish descent and a Methodist. When he was four, the family moved to Canada where his father became an Oxford County, Ontario farmer. He was educated at Plattsville. From 1877 to 1884 he worked in a Plattsville general store. Later he worked at Toronto, Montreal, Guelph, and then New York City. He came to Alberta in 1911, and settled in Edmonton where he became a prominent merchant. He served as an Edmonton Alderman. James Ramsey was returned as the Conservative member for Edmonton East in 1917. He sat in the Legislature for four years as an opposition member. In 1921 he was defeated at the polls and then retired from politics at the age of fifty-seven. Ramsey died in 1949.

[See: Blue- Alberta – Past and Present, (1924)]

Major Lee Redman

Born October 4, 1884 at Oil City, Ontario, son of D.B. Redman and his wife Annie M. Wilson. He was of ethnic English descent. Educated at

Petrolla, he attended the University of Manitoba, graduating in Law, and then continued his legal studied as London University and the Inns of Court, London. He came to Alberta in 1906 and settled at Calgary where he read law with the legal firm of Lougheed, Bennett, McLaws. He was admitted to the Alberta Bar in 1913. At the outbreak of World War I, he enlisted as an officer with the Calgary Rifles, 103rd Regiment, and was sent to Europe with the Canadian Expeditionary Force. He saw active service on the Western Front. He was seriously wounded in April 1915. Mayor D. Lee Redman was returned the Unionist Pro-Borden government member for the Calgary East Riding in 1917. He sat in the House of Commons for four years. In 1921 he did not seek re-election but retired from politics at the age of thirty-two. In 1922 he became a legal partner in the firm of Lougheed, McLars, Sinclair and Redman.

Ezra Hounsfield Riley

Born June 5 1866 at Toronto, Canada West, eldest son of Thomas Riley and his wife Georgina Jane Hannsfield. His father homesteaded near Calgary in 1888 and became a rancher. His younger brother was Harold W. H. Riley. He was of ethnic English descent and an Anglican. He was educated at Montreal. On the outbreak of the Northwest Revolt in 1885, he enlisted in the Montreal Rifle Militia and saw active service in the subsequent campaign. He became a Calgary rancher. Ezra H. Riley was returned the Liberal member for Gleichen in the 1906 by-election. He sat in the Legislature for four years. He vacated his seat in protest against the way the Chief Justice of Alberta (Arthur L. Sifton) was requested to become the premier and form a government by Lieutenant Governor G. H.V. Bulyea in what he considered a "most unparliamentary manner". He was defeated by Liberal Arthur J. McArthur in the October 3 1910 by-election and then retired from politics. He died January 5, 1937 at Calgary.

Harold William Hounsfield Riley

Born December 15, 1877 at Montreal son of Thomas Riley and his wife Georgina Jane Hannsfield. His brother was Ezra H. Riley. He was of ethnic English descent and an Anglican. Educated at Calgary. He became a Calgary investment dealer. In 1897, he married Alpha Maud

Keene of St. Mary's, Ontario. Their only son was Harold W. Riley, a.c., a Calgary Lawyer. (1903-1979). He was an unsuccessful federal Liberal candidate in 1953. In 1956, he was appointed a Justice of Alberta Supreme Court: Trial Division. He vacated the Bench in 1973. Justice Riley is still remembered as the ablest jurist of his generation! Harold W. H. Riley was returned as the Conservative member for Gleichen in the October 31, 1911 by-election. He sat in the Legislature for two years as an Opposition member. In 1913 he did not seek re-election but retired from politics at the age of thirty-five. He served as a city alderman and was the Deputy Provincial Secretary from 1905 until he resigned in 1910. He died in 1947.

Robert Melville Roberts

Born December 15, 1879 at Pedee, Cedar Country, Iowa, son of Scottish born parents. He was an Anglican. He attended the State University of Iowa, graduating in Law, and practiced in Iowa City. He came to Canada as a young man where he settled at High River establishing his law practice. Robert Melville Roberts was returned as the Liberal member for High River in 1909. He sat in the Legislature as a government backbencher for four years. In 1913 he did not seek re-election and retired from politics at the age of 33.

[See: Canadian Parliamentary Guide, (1913)]

Alberta John Robertson

Born September 17, 1864 at Markham, County York, Ontario, son of Henry Robertson and Mary Middleton. His father who was descended from the ancient earls of Athol, Scotland, was a graduate of Oxford. Educated at Markham and Weston, he attended McGill, graduating with a BA in 1895. He then went to Wesleyan Theological College, Montreal, obtaining a BD in 1895. He became a Methodist minister holding pastorates in the Maritimes and Illinois. He was a member of the Illinois Methodist Conference for several years before resigning from the Ministry in 1903. He served on the Conference for several years before resigning from the Ministry in 1903. He came to Alberta in 1903, where he became a Nanton farmer, merchant and real estate agent. He owned six sections of land in addition to two lumberyards.

A Conservative, Robertson owned six sections of land in addition to two lumberyards. A Conservative, Robertson contested successfully High River in 1905. He was one of the two Conservatives who contested successfully High River in 1905. He was one of the two Conservatives who were elected, and was the leader of the Opposition in the assembly for four years. He vocally supported the cause of Alberta obtaining control of her natural resources. He sat until defeated in Nanton in 1909 by Liberal J.M. Glendenning.

Anthony Sigwart de Rosenroll

Born December 4, 1857 at Castellamore, Italy, son of Rudolph de Rosenroll and his wife Margaret Thomson. He was born into a wealthy family. He was of ethnic Swiss-Scottish descent and a Presbyterian. Educated privately, he qualified as a land surveyor and civil engineer. He first worked as a land surveyor. He came to the Northwest Territories in 1890, settling at Wetaskiwin where he became a prominent Lumber Merchant and proprietor of a large stock and farmer near Wetaskiwin. Anthony S. De Rosenroll was returned as the Liberal member for Wetaskiwin in 1905. In 1909 he did not seek re-election but retired from politics at the age of fifty-two. He died May 8, 1945 at Wetaskiwin.

[See: MacRae. The History of Alberta, (1912)]

Alex Ross

Born January 15, 1880 at Premnoy, Scotland, song of James Ross and Jessie Thompson. He was of ethnic Scottish descent. Educated at Oynx, Aberdeenshire. He came to Canada as a young man in 1906, he settled at Calgary where he became a stonemason and was active in the trade union movement. Alex Ross was returned as the Labor member for Calgary Centre in 1917. He sat in the Legislature for nine years. In 1921 Premier Greenfield appointed Alex Ross to his U.F.A. cabinet as the Minister of Public Works. He held this portfolio for five years. In the 1926 general election Ross lost his seat in the Legislature.

Andrew Stefan Shandro

Born April 3 1886 in Bukowina, Austria, son of Stefan Shandro and his wife Nostansi Ostasheko. The family was wealthy. He was of ethnic Russian descent and a member of the Greek Orthodox Church. His grandfather was a judge while an uncle was a general. He came to Canada as a child in 1898, the family settled at Shandro, east of Edmonton. Young Shandro attended the Edmonton Business College. In 1905 he married Rose Hawrelak, daughter of Nicoli Hawrelak of Bukowing. They had six children. Pearl, one of his daughters, married William Hawrelak who died while Mayor of Edmonton in 1975. Andrew S. Shandro became a prominent farmer and a leader in the Ukrainian community. He served as a federal homestead inspector. Andrew S. Shandro was returned the Liberal member for Whitford in 1913. The courts declared the election void. He was re-elected in the March 15, 1915 by-election. He was re-elected because he was in the Canadian Army by act of the Legislature in 1917. In 1921 Shandro was re-elected by acclamation, however this election was declared void by the courts. He was defeated by Michael Horthus in the 1922 by-election. He was an unsuccessful candidate in 1926, 1930 and again in 1935. He died in 1942.

[See: Canadian Parliamentary Guide, (1922)]

Hugh Murray Shaw

Born November 13, 1876 at Kintone, Ontario, son of John Shaw and his wife Elizabeth Murray. He was of ethnic Scottish descent and a Presbyterian. Educated at Kinton His father moved the family to High River in 1891. Young Shaw completed his education in Calgary. He became a prominent Nanton farmer. He is credited with founding the Nanton community. Hugh M. Shaw was returned the Unionist Pro-Borden government member for the Macleod riding in 1917. He sat in the House of Commons for four years. In 1921 Shaw, running as a Conservative, was defeated in his re-eleciton bid by Progressive U.F.A. member George G. Cote. He then retired from politics at the age of forty-one. Shaw died April 3, 1934 at Calgary.

Robert Lee Shaw

Born November 27, 1865 at Roseburg, Oregon. He was an American of Scottish descent. As a young man from 1893 to 1897 he was employed as a cattle buyer for Portland Union Meat Company. He came to Canada as a cattle buyer in 1902, he settled at Stettler where he became a prominent businessman. He also was the proprietor of the Stettler National Hotel. Robert Lee Shaw was returned the Liberal member for Stettler in 1909. He sat in the Legislature for eight years as a government backbencher. In 1917 he did not seek re-election but retired from politics at the age of fifty-two.

William Charles Simmons

Born February 28, 1858 at Tara, Bruce County, Canada West, son of William Simmons and his wife Jane. He was of ethnic Scottish descent and a Presbyterian. Educated at Owen Sound, he attended the Toronto Normal School, qualifying as a teacher. He was the principal at Kent County Model School from 1892 to 1895. Later he taught at Chathan. He attended the University of Toronto, graduating in Arts in 1895. He came to the Northwest Territories in 1900 and settled at Cardston. Later he moved to Lethbridge where he served as crown prosecutor. He also was a partner in the legal firm of Simmons and Shepherd. William C. Simmons was returned the Liberal member for Lethbridge in the July 16, 1906 by-election. The vacancy had been caused by the incumbent Dr. L. George DeVeder when he was summoned to the Senate. Simmons vacated his seat in 1908 in order to enter federal politics. He was an unsuccessful Liberal candidate in the Medicine Hat riding in the October 26, 1908 general election. He lost to Charles A. McGrath. Shortly afterwards, he moved to Calgary. Justice Minister A.B. Aplesorth appointed Simmons a Justice of the Supreme Court in 1910. When the courts were re-organized in 1921, Justice Simmons was transferred to the Supreme Court: Trial Division. He was elevated to be the Chief Justice of the Supreme Court: Trial Division in 1924. He held this position for twelve years. Justice Simmons retired from the Bench in 1936. He died August 25, 1956 at Victoria, B.C.

[See: Mardon. Alberta Judicial Biographical Dictionary]

John A. Simpson

Born August 20, 1854 in Peel County, Canada West, son of William Simpson who had been born in Scotland. He was of ethnic Scottish descent and a Presbyterian. Educated at Calross, Bruce County. He came to the Northwest Territories in 1880, he settled near Innisfail where he became a well-known rancher and Innisfail merchant. John A. Simpson was returned as the member for Red Deer in 1894 and sat in the N.W.T. Assembly for eleven years until it went out of existence. Simpson was returned the Liberal member for Innisfail in 1905 and sat in the Alberta Legislature for eight years. In 1913 Conservative Red Archer defeated him. He then retired from politics at the age of fifty-nine. He died in 1916 at Innisfail.

George Skelding

He was of ethnic Scottish descent and a Presbyterian. He became a Fort MacLeod coal merchant. George Skelding was returned the Liberal member for MacLeod in 1917. He sat in the Legislature for four years as a government backbencher. In 1921 he was defeated by U.F.A. candidate W.H. Shields. He died in 1927 at Fort MacLeod.

George Peter Smith

Born August 26, 1873 at Middlesex County, Ontario, son of Peter Smith and his wife Hannah. He was of ethnic Scottish descent and Presbyterian. Educated at Strathroy, be attended the Toronto Normal School and qualified as a teacher in 1898. He then taught in Middlesex County. He came to the Northwest Territories in 1901, to become a general merchant, first at Duhamel, and then Camrose in 1906. Smith became the publisher of the Camrose Canadian. He served on the town council. George Peter Smith was returned as the Liberal member for Camrose in 1909 and sat in the Legislature for twelve years. Premier Sifton appointed him to the Cabinet as Provincial secretary in 1917. He was transferred to the Education Portfolio. In the 1921 election U.F.A. candidate V. Winfield Smith defeated him. G.P. Smith then returned to Ontario. He died in 1942.

George Douglas Stanley

Born March 19, 1876 at Exetor, Ontario, son of Thomas D. Stanley and his wife Hannah Westman. His family was wealthy. His father had served as the mayor of St. Mary's. He was of Anglo-Irish descent and a Methodist. Educated at St. Mary's Ontario, he attended the University of Toronto, graduating in Medicine. He came to the Northwest Territories where he settled at Calgary and became both a prominent surgeon, and also a strong prohibitionist. Later he moved to High River. He was an unsuccessful Conservative candidate in 1909. He served as chairman of the Board of Mount Royal College, Calgary. Dr. George D. Stanley was returned the Conservative member for High River in 1913. He sat in the Legislature as an Opposition member for eight years. In 1921 he did not seek re-election. Turning to federal politics, Dr. Stanley was returned the Conservative member for the Calgary East riding in 1930. He sat in the House of Commons as a government backbencher for five years. In 1935 he was defeated in his re-election bid by Social Creditor John C. Landeryou and then retired from politics. He died February 22, 1954. Dr. Stanley's nephew Is D. George F.G. Stanley, O.C., who served as the Lieutenant Government of New Brunswick from 1981-1987.

[See: Canadian's Who's Who, (1937)]

Joseph Ephraim State

Born June 15, 1867 at London, Ontario, son of James State and his wife Mary. He was ethnic Anglo-Irish descent. Educated at London, he attended the Detroit College of Medicine and Surgery, graduating with a medical degree. He arrived in the Northwest Territories and settled at Edmonton, where he became a well-known physician. Dr. Joseph Ephraim State was returned as the Liberal member for Clearwater in 1917. He sat in the Legislature until the time of his death. He died in 1924 while still a sitting member at the age of fifty-seven. Rather then hold a by-election, the Legislature passed legislation that abolished the Clearwater Constituency.

[See: Canadian Parliamentary Guide, (1924)]

Joseph Emmett Stauffer

Born October 29, 1874 at Mannasar, Virginia, son of Benjamin Sauffer and his wife Mary Betzner. He was of ethnic German-Swiss descent and a Presbyterian. Is ancestors immigrated to the Colony of Pennsylvania in 1712. During the American Revolution, the Stauffers were true to the Old Flag and after the war became United Empire Loyalists at Waterloo, Upper Canada. He came to Canada as a child with his parents, and was educated at Berlin (later Kitchener), Ontario. He attended Ottawa Normal School qualifying as a teacher in 1900. He then taught school in Waterloo County. He came to the Northwest Territories in 1902 where he settled at Didsbury and he taught a year before becoming a federal homestead inspector. He left the civil service to become a farmer and real estate agent. J. Emmett Stauffer was returned the Liberal member for Didsbury in 1909. He sat in the Legislature for eight years. He served as the Deputy Speaker. On the outbreak of World War I, he enlisted in the Canadian Army. He went overseas as a Lieutenant with the 49th Battalion with the Canadian Expeditionary Force. Lt. Stauffer was killed in action in the battle for Vimy Ridge, April 1917.

[See: MacRae. The History of Alberta, (1912)]

Charles Allen Stuart

Born August 3 1864 at Middlesex County Ontario, son of Charles Stuart, a prominent Caradox farmer. He was of ethnic Scottish descent and a Presbyterian. He attended the University of Toronto, graduating in Classics. He became a lecturer in Constitution History at the University of Toronto while he attended Toronto's Osgoode Hall Haw School. Stuart was admitted to the Ontario Bar. He only practiced law briefly at Toronto before he became ill. He moved to Mexico for a year to recover. Afterwards, he practiced with the legal firm of McCarthy and Stuart. He was an unsuccessful N.W.T. Assembly candidate in 1900. Later he joined the Legal firm of Sifton, Short and Start. He took a prominent part in the formation of the Alberta Liberal Party in 1905. Charles A. Stuart was returned the Liberal member for Gleichen in the first provincial general election in November 1905. He sat in the Legislature for one year. He vacated his seat on his appointed as a Justice of the N.W.T. Supreme Court on October 6, 1906. A year later he was transferred to the newly created Alberta Supreme Court. In 1921 he retired from the Bench.

[See: Who's Who and Why, (1912)]

Charles Stewart (Premier)

Born August 26, 1868 at Strathbane, Ontario, son of Charles Stewart and his wife Catherine. He was of Scottish descent and an Anglican. He came to Alberta where he homesteaded in the Killam district. Charles Stewart was retuned as the Liberal member for Sedgewick in 1989 and he sat in the Legislature for the next thirteen years. He served Minister of Municipal Affairs and Minister of Public Works. In 1917, when Premier A.L. Sifton resigned his seat in the Legislature on his appointment to the federal cabinet, Stewart succeeded him in the premiership. He was premier from 1917-1921. In 1922 he vacated his seat to enter federal politics. Charles Stewart was first returned as Liberal member for the federal riding of Argeneuil, Quebec in the by-election of March 1922 and then from 1925 to 1935 as the Liberal member for the Edmonton West riding. 1921 he was appointed Minister for the Interior by Prime Minister Mackenzie King. He held the portfolio until 1930. In 1935 he was unsuccessful in his bid to be returned as the member for Jasper-Edson and retired from politics at the age of 67. He died December 1946 at Ottawa. His grandson is Charles Stewart.

[See: Canadian Who's Who, (1935)]

John Smith Stewart

Born May 18, 1878 at Brampton, Ontario, son of John Stewart and his wife Mary Armstrong. He was of ethnic Scottish descent and a Methodist. Educated at Brampton, he attended the University of Toronto, graduating in dentistry in 1903. Previously he saw active service with Lord Strathcona House in the South African War (Boer War). Upon his arrival in the Northwest Territories he settled at Lethbridge where he practiced dentistry for more than sixty years. He was also active in the militia. During World War I, he served as an artillery officer with the Canadian Expeditionary Force. He rose to the rank for Brigadier

General and was the commander of the 1919 Siberian Expeditionary Force. Dr. John S. Stewart was returned the Conservative member for Lethbridge City in October 31, 1911 by-election. He sat in the Legislature for fourteen years. He vacated his seat to unsuccessfully run for Parliament in 1925. Dr. Stewart was returned the Conservative member for Lethbridge riding in 1930. He sat in the House of Commons for five years as a government backbencher. In 1935 Social Creditor Jon H. Blackmore defeated him. He then retired to his dental practice at the age of fifty-seven. He died in 1970.

[See: Canadian Who's Who, (1967)]

Peter Talbot

Born March 30, 1854 at Eramosa, Canada West, son of Henry Talbot and his wife Margaret Stewart. He was of ethnic Scottish descent. He was also a Freemason. Educated at Rockwood, he attended the Ottawa Normal School qualifying as a teacher. He then became a rural teacher. He came to the Northwest Territories in 1890 and settled at Fort MacLeod where he served as the principal of the high school. Two years later, he homesteaded near Lacombe where he became a prominent farmer. He started the first store in Lacombe. Peter Talbot was returned as the Member for Lacombe in the Northwest Assembly in 1902. He sat in the Assembly for two years before he vacated his seat. Turning to Federal politics Talbot was returned as the Liberal member for this Strathcona riding in 1904. He sat in the House of Commons for two years before he vacated his seat. Turning to federal politics Talbot was returned as the Liberal member for the Strathcona riding in 1904. He sat in the House of Commons for two years before he was summoned to the Senate on March 8, 1906. He had previously refused Prime Minister Laurier's offer to be the first Premier of Alberta due to poor health. He died December 6, 1919 at Lacombe Alberta.

[See: Canadian Parliamentary Guide, (1919)]

Robert Taylor Telford

Born June 18 1860 at Bryson, Lower Canada, son of Robert Telford and his wife Ann Pratt. His father was an Ottawa valley farmer who had come from Ireland in 1845. He was educated at Bryson. He travelled and worked in the United States for several years. He came to the Northwest Territories as a member of the Northwest Mounted Police in 1885. He served in the force for four years. After his discharge he established a staging post one day's ride south of Strathcona. He became a prominent lumber merchant. The settlement was known as Telfordville. Later the government changed the name to Leduc, to honor Rev. Hippolyte Leduc, O.M.I., the Catholic missionary. Telford was the first postmaster. Robert T. Telford was returned the Liberal member for election but retired from politics. Telford died in 1933.

[See: Who's Who and Why, (1910)]

James Gray Turgeon

Born October 7, 1879 at Bathurst, New Brunswick, son of Onesiphone Turgeon, long-time editor of the Le Courier des Proviacer Maritimes (1871-1921), and Margaret Eulalia Baldivin. His father was a prominent Liberal Member of Parliament from 1900 to 1921 and a Senator from 1922 to 1944. His elder brother, William Ferdinand Alphonse Turgeon who served as the Saskatchewan attorney general from 1907-1921, later he was Saskatchewan's Chief Justice before becoming the Canadian ambassador to Argentine, Belgium. He was educated at Bathurst and New York. He came to Alberta in 1907, settling at Hardisty where he became a financial agent for the next twenty years. In 1909 he married Emma Bondreau, formerly of Petit Rocher, New Brunswick. They had two sons and two daughters. He was a French Canadian Roman Catholic. Interested in provincial politics, James Gray Turgeon, running as a Liberal, successfully contested Ribstone in 1913. He sat in the Legislature for eight years as a private member on the government side of the House. In the 1921 Alberta election, he was defeated by C.O.F. Wright, the U.F.A. candidate by a 1,283 vote margin. In 1930, he moved to British Columbia and settled in Vancouver. Turning to British Columbia politics, James Gray Turgeon unsuccessfully contested Vancouver East in 1933. Turning to Federal politics, James Grey Turgeon, running as a Liberal, successfully contested the Caribou riding in the 1935 general election. He was re-elected in the 1940 general election. Turgeon sat for ten years in the House of Commons. In 1936 he was appointed Deputy Government Whip. In the 1945 general election, he was defeated by William Irvine, a former

Member of Parliament for Calgary by a 932 vote margin. Prime Minister MacKenzie King appointed James Gray to the Senate on January 27, 1947. He died February 14, 1964 at Vancouver at the age of eighty-four.

[See: Canadian's Who's Who, (1961)]

Thomas Mitchell March Tweedie

Born March 4, 1872 at River John, Nova Scotia, song of James Tweedie and his wife Ruth smith. He was of Scottish descent and a Methodist. He attended Mount Allison University, graduating in Arts. He then moved to the States where he attended Harvard University. He was admitted to the Nova Scotia Bar in 1905. Upon arrival in Alberta he settled at Calgary where he became a prominent lawyer. He was a legal partner of A.A. McGilivrey. Thomas M.M. Tweedie was returned as Conservative member for Calgary Centre in the October 1911 by-election. He sat in the Legislature for six years. Labor candidate Alex Ross defeated him in the 1917 Alberta election. In the December 1917 Alberta election, Tweedie was returned the Unionist member for Calgary West. He sat in the House of Common for four years as a government backbencher. On his appointment to the Bench in September 1921 he vacated his seat. He was a Justice of the Alberta Supreme Court: Trial Division for death. Chief Justice Tweedie died October 4, 1944 at Lethbridge.

[See: Canadian Who's Who, (1938)]

Frank Austin Walker

Born November 17, 1871 at Lucan, Ontario, son of William Walker and Catherine Spencer. He was an Anglican of Anglo-Irish descent. He came to western Canada as a child and was educated in Winnipeg and Edmonton. He became a prominent Fort Saskatchewan merchant and real estate agent. During World War I he served as an officer and went overseas with the Canadian Expeditionary Force. He saw active service on the Western Front. Frank A. Walker was returned to the first Alberta Legislature as the Liberal member for the Victoria constituency. He sat in the chamber as a government backbencher for sixteen years. United Farmers of Alberta candidate, William Fedun, defeated him in 1921. He then retired from politics at the age of 50. He died in 1956.

Dr. David E. Warnock

Born April 11, 1885 at Hampton, Lunakshire Scotland, son of George Warnock and his wife Janet Finlay. He was of ethnic Scottish descent and a Presbyterian. Educated at Hamilton, he qualified as a veterinary surgeon. Upon arrival in the Northwest Territories, he was a federal veterinary inspector of animals at Contts, Alberta from 1904 to 1909. He then became a farmer. Dr. David E. Warnock was returned the Liberal member for Pincher Creek in 1909. He sat in the Legislature for two years. During the Railway Scandal debate, he was a leader until the Liberal "insurgents" who attacked Premier Rutherford's handling of the Great Water ways Railway Contracts. In 1911 he vacated his seat to enter federal politics. Dr. Warnock was returned the Liberal member for MacLeod riding in the 1911 federal election. He sat in the House of Commons for six years as an Opposition member. In 1917 he did not seek re-election but retired from politics.

James Weir

Born August 5 1853 at Elginfield, Middlesex County, Ontario, son of Robert Weir and his wife Martha Sutton. He was of Ulster Scot descent and a Presbyterian. His grandfather had been a pioneer settler in Upper Canada. Educated at Windsor, he became a newspaper editor at Hamilton and later at Windsor. Upon arrival in the Northwest Territories, he became a Saskatoon publisher before finally settling at Strathcona. Later he became a prominent Parkland famer south of Calgary. He was active in the formation of the United Farmers of Alberta movement. James Weir was returned the Non-Partician League member for Nanton in 1917. He sat in the Legislature as an independent farmer for four years. In 1921 he did not seek re-election but retired from politics

William Henry 'Nobby' White

Born August 21, 1865 at City View, Canada West, son of John White and Sarah McAmmond. He was of English-Scottish descent and an Anglican. Educated at Ottawa. He came to the Northwest Territories as a young man in 1881 to enlist in the Northwest Mounted Police. He served for six year with the Force and saw active service in the Northwest rebellion in 1885. After resigning, he became a farmer-rancher near Fort Saskatchewan. W.H. 'Nobby' White was returned as the member for Victoria (Alberta) riding in 1908. He sat in the Commons for 13 years. In the 1917 wartime federal election, White was the only anti-conscription Laurier candidate to be elected in Alberta. The other 11 elected members were Pro-Borden Unionist. At the time it was said that a large number of voters in the Victoria riding had been born in Scandinavia, or the German or Austrian empires. Few spoke English. In 1921 White did not seek re-election and retired form politics at the age of 56. He died June 1930 at Fort Saskatchewan.

[See: Who's Who and Why, (1912)]

Frank Henry Whiteside

Born July 15, 1873 at Ottawa, Ontario, son of Henry Whiteside and his wife Hannah L. Stone. His father was a St. John customs official for fifty years. He was of ethnic English descent and of United Empire Loyalist stock and a Methodist. Educated at St. John Commercial College. He spent time in British Columbia as a young man. He came to the Northwest Territories in 1894, settling near Red Deer where he became a homesteader. Later he became a Stettler farmer. In 1908 he established himself as a Coronation farmer and publisher of the Coronation Review. Frank H. Whiteside was returned as the Liberal member for Coronation in 1913. He sat in the Legislature as a government backbencher until the time of his death. In spring 1916 Whiteside and Helmbolt, a friend and his campaign manager, enlisted at Calgary and trained with the 187th Battalion. They were both scheduled to go overseas. Both privates returned to Coronation on leave in September. During an argument Whiteside was shot in both arms by Pte. Helbolt. At first the injuries did not appear of a serious nature. However, gangrene set in and both of Whiteside's arms had to be amputated. He died October 4, 1916. Premier Sifton attended his funeral. In November 1916 the trial of Pte. Helmbolt on the charge of murder of the member of the Legislature was held at Stettler. They jury returned a verdict of 'not guilty'.

Conrad Widerhammer

Born January 27, 1866 near St. Clemons, Ontario son of Christopher Widerhammer, a farmer and his wife Mary Annie Brodbeck. He was of ethnic German descent. He married Eva Elisa Ebel and was educated at Semira. As a young man, he came to the Northwest Territories and homesteaded near Spruce Grove, west of Edmonton. A large number of Germans settled here and at Stony Plain. In time he became a prominent farmer. He was an unsuccessful candidate in 1905. Conrad Wiederhammer was returned as the Conservative member for Stony Plain in 1913. He sat in the Legislature for four years as an Opposition member. In 1917 he did not seek re-election but retired from politics at the age of fifty-one.

[See: Canadian Parliamentary Guide, (1917)]

William W. Wilson

He became a prominent Coronation farmer. He was an unsuccessful candidate in 1913. William W. Wilson was returned as the Conservative member for Coronation in 1917. He sat in the Legislature for four years as an opposition member. In 1921 he did not seek re-election but retired from politics.

[See: Canadian Parliamentary Guide, (1921)]

John William Woolf

Born on November 27, 1868 at Hyde Park, Utah, the song of Absalom Woolf and Harriet Wood. His paternal grandfather, John A. Woolf, born in upstate New York, joined the Mormon church soon after its organization. His ancestor was among the first pioneers to cross the plains and to establish Salt Lake City in 1847. Jon W. Woolf's elder brother was Martin Woolf (1858-1928). Educated at Hyde Park, he attended Logan College, in Logan, Utah. Coming to the district of Alberta, Northwest Territories he was among the first Mormon settlers in 1887. He played a key role in the establishment of the Cardston Mercantile Company. Active in community affairs, he served on the first Cardston town council in 1904. Because of rapid growth of the Mormon settlement, it became entitled to send an elected representative to the Northwest Territorial Legislative Assembly. Elected as a Liberal candidate, John W. Woolf was returned as the member for the newly created Cardston Constituency in 1902. He was re-elected to the first Alberta Legislature in 1911. He seat was declared vacant by the Legislature in 1912. In the subsequent by-election, John's older brother, Martin Woolf, was returned. The Cardston seat remained with the Woolf family for nineteen years. Woolf died February 23, 1950 at Salt Lake City at the age of 82.

[See: Mardon. Alberta Mormon Politicians, (1992)]

Martin Woolf

Born October 18, 1858, at Hyde Park, Utah, the song of Absalom Woolf and Harriet Wood. His parents had come to Utah during the famous 'Mormon Trek' overland across the great plains to the Salt Lake Valley in 1847. His father was a veteran of the Black Hawk Indian War. Raised on a farm, Martin Woolf was educated at Cache County schools at Utah, before attending Bringham Young College. He qualified as a teacher, serving as the principal of Millville school for 15 years. Arriving in Alberta in 1899, he homesteaded west of Cardston. He was secretary-treasurer to the new town and in 1909 he was named a customs official and federal land agent. A Liberal, he entered politics when the Cardston provincial constituency was declared vacated, because his brother John Woolf moved permanently to the United States. He won the May 12, 1912 Cardston Provincial Constituency by-election. He was named the deputy-speaker of the provincial legislature in 1919. He sat until defeated in 1921 by George Stringham, the U.F.A. candidate. He was an able debater and an outspoken advocate of prohibition. In 1880 he married Rose Hyde. They had three children. He was a councilor by Bishop hammer of the Cardston Ward. He died August 25, 1928 at Cardston at the age of 70.

[See: Mardon. Alberta Mormon Politicians, (1992)]

GENERAL INDEX OF ALBERTA POLITICIANS 1905-1921

Archer, Frederick W. (Innisfail)
Atkins, Henry B.
Barker, G. Russell (Lac St. Anne)
Bennett, R.B. (Calgary)
Blair, William J.
Blow, Dr. Thomas H. (Calgary)
Boudreau, Lucien (St. Albert)
Boyle, John R. (Sturgeon)
Bramley-Moore, Alwyn A. (Alexandra)
Bredin, W. Fletcher (Athabasca)
Brett, Dr. R.G.
Brick, T. Allie (Peace River)
Buchanan, William A. (Lethbridge)
Bulyea, G.H.V.
Campbell, Archibald (Vermillion)
Campbell, Robert D. (Rocky Mountain House)
Campbell, Mr. William A. (Ponoka)
Clark, Dr. Michael
Cornwall, "Peace River Jim" (Peace River)
Cote, Jean-Leon (Grouard)
Crawford, Herbert H. (Edmonton South)
Cross, Charles W. (Edson)
Cunningham, Charles O. (Ponoka)
Cushing, William H. (Calgary)
Vadidson, William M. (Calgary North)
Davis Fred (Glechem)
DeVeber, Dr. L. George (Lethbridge)
Douglas, James M.
Dubuc, Lucien (Peace River)
Eaton, R.B. (Hand Hills)
Ebbett, A.W. (Vermillion)
Ewing, Alfred F. (Edmonton)
Finly, William t. (Medicine Hat)
Risher, Charles W. (Chocrane)
Forget, A.
Gaetz, John Jost (Red Deer)
Gardiner, Robert

Gariepy, Wilfred (Beaver River)
Gilmour, Andrew (Lacombe)
Glendenning, John M. (Nanton)
Griesbach, William A.
Gunn, Peter (Lac St. Anne)
Hallway, Howard H.
Hamrer, James W.
Heron, John
Hieert, Cornelious (Rosebud)
Hillocks, S. Bacon (Calgary North)
Hoadley, George (Okotoks)
Holden, James B. (Vegreville)
Hudson, G.E. Leron (Wainwright)
Kemmis, John H.W.S. (Pincher Creek)
Lane, George (Bow Valley)
Leffinwell, Prosper E. (St. Paul)
Lougheed, J.A.
Lowery, James R. (Alexandra)
Lundy, Frederick W. (Stony Plain)
MacAdams, Lt. Roberta L. (Overseas Soldiers)
McArthur, A.J. (Gleichen)
McArthur, J.P. (Gleichen)
McCarthy, M.S.
McCauley, Matthew (Vermiilion)
McColl, John A. (Acadia)
McDougall, J.A. (Edmonton)
MacDonald, Gordon (Pembina)
McIntyre, Dr. Wilbert
MacKay, Alexander G. (Athabasca)
Kenny, Henry (Clearwater)
McKenny, Mrs. Louise C. (Clareholm)
McKenzie, Malcolm (MacLeod)
Mackie, Arthur H.
McLean, Archibald J. (Taber)
McLeod, Dr. John R. (Ponoka)
McNabb, Donald (Lethbridge)
McNaughton, James (Little Bow)
McPherson, J.A. (Stony Plain)
Magrath, Charles A.
Marcellus, John P. (Pincher Creek)
Marshall, Duncan M. (Olds)

Michener, E. (Red Deer)
Mills, G.S. (Athabasca)
Mitchell, Judge Charles R. (Bow Valley)
Moffatt, William (Claresholm)
Montgomery, Hugh John (Wetaskiwin)
Moore, Alexander (Cochrane)
Moore, John T. (Red Deer)
Morkberg, Daniel J. (Innisfail)
O'Brien, Charles H. (Rocky Mountain)
Olin, Charles H. (Wetaskiwin)
Oliver Frank
Patterson, Alphonse (Peace River)
Patterson, Robert
Pearson, Captain Robert (Overseas Soldiers)
Pingle, Charles S. (Redcliff)
Prudden, Edward H. (Stettler)
Puffer, William F. (Lacombe)
Rae, W. Archibald (Peace River)
Ramsey, James (Edmonton East)
Redman, D. Lee
Riley, Ezra H. (Gleichen)
Riley, H.W.H. (Gleichen)
Robert, Louis M. (High River)
Robertson, A. J. (High River)
Rosenroll, Anthony S. (Wetaskiwin)
Ross, Alex (Calgary Centre)
Rutherford, Alexander (Strathcona)
Roy, Dr. Phillipe
Scott, David Lynch
Shandro, Andrew S. (Whitford)
Shaw, Hugh M.
Shaw, Robert L. (Stettler)
Sifton, Arthur Lewis (Vermillion)
Simmons, William C. (Lethbridge)
Simpson, John A. (Stony Plain)
Skelding, George (MacLeod)
Smith, George P. (Camrose)
Spencer, Nelson (Medicine Hat)
Stanley, Dr. George D. (High River)
State, Dr. J. Ephraim (Clearwater)
Stauffer, J. Emmett (Didsbury)

Stewart, Charles A. (Sedgewick)
Stewart, Dr. John S. (Lethbridge)
Stuart, Charles (Gleichen)
Talbot, Peter
Telford, Robert T. (Leduc)
Tobin, Stanley G. (Leduc)
Turgeon, J. Grey (Ribstone)
Tweedie, T.M.M. (Calgary)
Walker, Frank A. (Victoria)
Warnock, Dr. David (Pincher Creek)
Weir, James (Nanton)
White, W.H. 'Nobby'
Whiteside, Frank H. (Coronation)
Widerhammer, Conrad (Stony Plain)
Wilson, William W. (Coronation)
Woolf, J.W. (Cardston)
Woolf, Martin (Cardston)

Acknowledgements

Any study of this sort is dependent upon the support and efforts of a wide variety of people. The authors would like to thank the staff at the Provincial Archives of Alberta, the Legislative Library of Alberta, and the Office of the Chief Electoral Officer of Alberta for all of their assistance and encouragement. They would also like to thank staff of the Historic Sites and Archives Serve, Alberta Community Development, including Carl Betke, Les Hurt, Michael Payne, Hannah Aaron, Lynn Pong and Dawna Manderson, for their help in preparing this manuscript for publication and for their support of the project. A special thanks to the Documentary Heritage Society of Alberta, which agreed on short notice to co-publish this volume, is also in order.

Finally the financial assistance given to this project by the Senate of the University of Alberta through the Skarin Award Foundation is gratefully acknowledged.

www.ingramcontent.com/pod-product-compliance
Lightning Source LLC
Chambersburg PA
CBHW031555300426
44111CB00006BA/323